Nightmare on Iwo Jima

A Marine in Combat

Patrick F. Caruso

With a New Foreword by David G. Rathgeber

THE UNIVERSITY OF ALABAMA PRESS

Tuscaloosa

Copyright © 2001
Foreword and Index copyright © 2007
The University of Alabama Press
Tuscaloosa, Alabama 35487-0380
All rights reserved
Manufactured in the United States of America

Originally Published by Naval Institute Press

First paperback printing 2007

∞
The paper on which this book is printed meets the minimum requirements of
American National Standard for Information Science—Permanence of Paper for
Printed Library Materials, ANSI Z39.48-1984.

Library of Congress Cataloging-in-Publication Data

Caruso, Patrick F., 1921—
  [Nightmare on Iwo]
  Nightmare on Iwo Jima / a marine in combat / Patrick F. Caruso.
     p. cm.
     "Fire Ant books."
  Originally published as: Nightmare on Iwo. Annapolis, Md. : Naval Institute
Press, 2001.
  Includes bibliographical references and index.
  ISBN-13: 978-0-8173-5448-0 (pbk. : alk. paper)
  ISBN-10: 0-8173-5448-4 (alk. paper)
  1. Caruso, Patrick F., 1921— 2. Iwo Jima, Battle of, Japan, 1945—Personal
narratives, American. 3. World War, 1939—1945—Regimental histories—
United States. 4. United States. Marine Corps. Division, 3rd. Battalion, 3rd. Kilo
Company—History. 5. Iwo Jima (Volcano Islands, Japan)—History, Military—
20th century. 6. United States. Marine Corps—Officers—Biography. I. Title.
  D767.99.I9C37 2007
  940.54'2528092—dc22
                                    2007008352

Nightmare on Iwo Jima

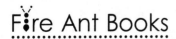
Fire Ant Books

To all of the men and women killed in America's wars

For all the Graces and Blessings
God has handed . . .
May we not take them for granted.

Contents

The battle for Iwo Jima, which took place over fifty years ago, is still the battle that many believe defines today's Marine Corps. Iwo Jima is the only battle in Marine Corps history where U.S. casualties outnumbered the enemy's. There were no great or grand tactics. The fight was measured in feet and yards, with the enemy fighting from a maze of interconnecting tunnels from which he could see but not be seen.

K Company, Third Battalion, Ninth Marine Regiment, Third Marine Division, landed with the third wave. Within one hour of their initial assault, a young second Lieutenant, formerly sixth on the company's chain of command, found himself thrust to the fore and required to take the responsibilities of company commander. When it was over, only 40 of the original 230 men in the company remained, and 100 percent of the officers were killed or wounded, including the young lieutenant. Patrick Caruso, the author, is that lieutenant.

Wounded on the fourteenth day of the battle, Caruso was evacuated to a hospital in Guam.

There he realized that his mind wanted to forget what he had seen and experienced and that faces and names were becoming difficult to remember. Caruso desperately wanted to keep alive the names and actions of all those who participated, so he began writing his recollections on any paper he could find; hospital napkins, paper bags, hospital reports, or anything else on which he could write were fair game for his notes. After the war, his wife typed the notes and put them away.

In 1970, Caruso wrote an article for the Associated Press as a commemoration of the twenty-fifth anniversary of the battle of Iwo Jima. The response to his article was tremendous. He received so many letters and calls from the men who were there or from their families that he decided to write a book.

Caruso's story is not about tactics or military strategy; it is a story of ordinary men in extraordinary circumstances. Caruso tells what happened in a matter-of-fact style, as he saw it, as he experienced it, and as in-depth as he could. Of particular interest are the vignettes he adds throughout the book. Various chapters cover specific actions and the individuals who were key players. After Caruso tells the story in his words, he often adds the recollection of survivors who took part in the action. This literary device could be distracting, but here it works. The reader is introduced to these remarkable men in an individual, personal way.

If you are interested in tactics and strategy, this book is not for you; however, if you are interested in the thoughts and feelings of the men who fought in this incredibly costly battle, you will find *Nightmare on Iwo Jima* fascinating and satisfying.

LTC David G. Rathgeber, USMC, Retired

Preface

As a retired American history teacher and school administrator, I have observed that the treatment of historical events is altered by the prevailing temperament of the times. Rewriting American history has become commonplace; the original account of an event may eventually be changed beyond recognition.

Therefore, it is of extreme importance that the facts of a historical event remain untampered with and intact for ages to come. To assure this, recorded facts should be derived from participants and prime witnesses to such events, not from versions rendered by distant observers, correspondents decades after the fact, or future generations that may not record such events accurately. To this end, I have written this account depicting my experiences and those of individual men in combat on Iwo Jima, the U.S. Marine Corps' costliest battle of the Pacific war—relying directly on those who fought there.

As a second lieutenant of K Company, Third Battalion, Ninth Regiment of the Third Marine

Division, I engaged in combat against the Japanese stronghold of Iwo Jima, participating in that conflict as a rifle company officer from early in the fight until I was wounded fifteen days after our battalion had landed.

As I lay on my back in a hospital bed on Guam one week later, I realized that my recollection of some of the events that had occurred during my fifteen days of combat was becoming vague. My senses had been put to the test on that island by the stench of the honorable dead; the lingering, penetrating odor of earth-shattering shells; the weird whistling of ricochet; the piercing shrill of buzz bombs; the horrible, agonizing cry of a wounded Marine calling for a medical corpsman; the stirring sight of those determined men who fell to a permanent position of death in their last step toward the enemy; the cruddy feel of the island's filthy black ash that clung to my skin. Now these senses were beginning to fade.

Also escaping my memory were the insecurity of not knowing which step would be my last; the jittery, sleepless, cold nights that seemed never to bring daylight; that religious feeling that is embedded in all men but which often requires the conditions of violent combat to draw it to the surface. I was becoming complacent and felt uncomfortable about it.

I was sleeping in a clean bed and receiving good medical attention. I was enjoying wholesome food, a treat after those stale crackers, processed water, hard candy, and rations. No longer were there shell blasts causing me to jump automatically to the nearest crater. Now I could wash, shave, and brush my teeth—all day long if I pleased. The nights were no longer nightmares, but served to provide hours of much-needed, restful sleep. Yet, I felt guilty, guilty because the fighting was still going on. I was resting and my buddies were still there.

There had been no greenery on Iwo, only black volcanic ash, odious sulfur deposits, and rugged black rocks on the island's northern end. Now I could see vegetation from my hospital bed. Until now, I had not known the full meaning of the word grateful. Dear Lord, may I never forget it!

Until now, anything that had come to my mind about the fighting had appeared so frightfully vivid that I lived through my ordeal again and again. But I was beginning to forget the reality and the men, and I wanted so much *not* to forget. No one wants to recall the vicious desecration of the sanctity of human life, but to allow myself to forget the deeds of our fallen brothers would be, I felt, an injustice and a breach to their memory.

There in that hospital, I decided to put these memories on paper before they vanished completely from my mind. It was all over for me. The question no longer was, "If I get back home." Rather, it was, "When I get back."

Feeling compelled to keep alive and nurture what I had observed and felt on Iwo Jima and to recall how many of my comrades had lost their lives, I jotted notes on whatever paper I could muster from the nurses: discarded hospital reports, paper bags, stationery, even napkins. These were to serve as reminders to bolster my fading recollections.

After the war, my wife, Mary, typed my rough notes, which eventually became the nucleus of this book. The notes remained dormant for years. In 1970, as the twenty-fifth anniversary of the campaign approached, I resurrected and organized them and submitted them to the Associated Press in New York City, whose photographer, Joe Rosenthal, had snapped the famous photograph of the raising of the American flag on Iwo Jima's Mt. Suribachi. I felt that the AP would be the logical publisher for my account because of this singular identity.

AP used my article to commemorate the anniversary. It was released to its member newspapers and appeared as a full-page spread throughout the country and overseas. The story generated more than one hundred phone calls and letters, some from the men I had mentioned in the article. The renewed contact with my Marine buddies led to the inevitable reunion of K Company survivors in St. Louis, Missouri, then the next year in Memphis, Tennessee, followed by Dallas, Texas. By that time, our group had increased to thirty men plus some wives and family members. Today the reunions have become an annual event, meeting in different locations across the United States. Through them, I have been able to collect many of the survivors' remembrances; many are contained in these pages.

The glow of Iwo Jima is fading. The roll call of those who survived the ordeal is rapidly diminishing; as I write this, the U.S. Department of Veterans Affairs estimates that 35,000 veterans of World War II die each month; that amounts to 420,000 annually.

It is not only appropriate but imperative that future generations reflect on the personal and human aspects of combat in addition to the inanimate and mundane summaries of statistical figures, such as the number of ships and planes, tons of bombs, reinforced concrete bunkers, and the like. Therefore, I have focused on the man of Iwo Jima—their reactions in combat; their emotions, hopes, anxieties, concerns, worries, hurts, joys, laughter, sacrifices, fears, and resolve; their deeds and their stress. By doing so, it is my hope that this book will ignite the flame for posterity and extol the deeds of the wounded and the dead who battled there, blending my recollections with those of the men who fought there during that nightmare in hell.

Part 1

A New Assignment

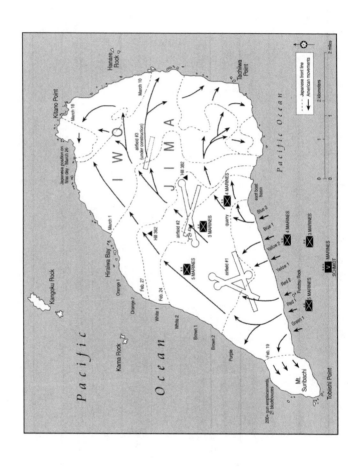

Chapter 1

The Preparation

T he battle on Guam was over and the island was secured, but the Third Marine Division remained for training exercises. After a few months we realized we would soon be called upon for the next campaign. This became evident when our training tempo was stepped up and they began to feed us better. A few days later we were notified that the division was designated to move out, but no one knew where or when we were going. We surmised it would be north of Guam toward Japan, where it was notably colder. Since our training had been geared to open-area fighting, we reasoned that our next assignment would not involve jungle warfare.

I had joined the Marine Corps after the Japanese attack on Pearl Harbor. On that fateful day, December 7, 1941, I was enrolled in the Army ROTC at Western Maryland College in Westminster, Maryland. Along with others my age, I realized that military service was now inevitable. I had to decide in which branch I would serve my country. As a member of the Army ROTC, I was eligible to remain in the program until

I received my commission. But that was two years away, and I felt the war would be over before I'd have the chance to get into it. The Army ROTC was out of the question and I did not want to wait to be drafted.

On December 8, 1941, the Japanese attacked tiny Wake Island, some two thousand miles west of Hawaii. Wake Island, our naval station, was guarded by a small detachment of Marines under the command of Maj. James Devereux of Maryland. The Marines courageously and stubbornly had repelled wave after wave of the invading forces. Without any hope of reinforcements or help from the outside world and greatly outnumbered, the Marines, by their dauntless spirit and determination, fought off the fierce enemy for two weeks. They just refused to surrender.

I remember listening intently to the radio for reports on the progress of our defense of Wake Island. As Christmas approached, Major Devereux was asked by radio if there was anything he would like for Christmas. His reply became the headline for days, "Send me more Japs." Wow, what bold valor, what courage, what zeal, what grit, I thought. His statement propelled all America to a pitch of patriotic frenzy. It stirred the blood in America's veins. It certainly did in mine.

On December 23, Japanese forces eventually captured the island, but it cost them the destruction of two destroyers, twenty-one aircraft, and almost twelve hundred casualties. We lost 120 men. The heroic defense of Wake Island provided the nation a glow of optimism and resolve to offset a bit of the smoldering disaster of Pearl Harbor. I decided then to drop out of the Army ROTC and enlist in the United States Marine Corps.

The following morning I hitchhiked from the college to the Marine Corps recruiting office in Washington, D.C. I'll never forget Captain Slaughter, who interviewed me. I liked his manner, and his name seemed appropriate for the Corps. He assured me that I would have no problem if I were to drop from the Army ROTC to enlist in the Marine Corps. Though still on active duty, I would have to wait until the end of the school year to be called. The Corps had enough recruits and was not taking anyone out of college in the middle of the school year. Thus I waited and waited.

I finally received my orders and was assigned to Bucknell University in Lewisburg, Pennsylvania, as part of a preliminary training to qualify for officers candidate school. We were trained by drill instructors and officers. The program was a form of pre-boot camp, and we were allowed to participate in the university's college activities. As a serviceman, I played football for Bucknell and that helped to ease the pain of waiting for advanced training. Near the end of the football season the wait was over and I was shipped to boot camp at Parris Island, South Carolina.

After basic training, I was recommended for consideration to officers candidate training and sent to candidate school at Quantico, Virginia, and then on to reserve officers training, which led to a commission as second lieutenant six months later. In June 1944, after further training at Camp Lejeune, North Carolina, I joined a replacement group for overseas at Camp Pendleton, California, where I learned that a transport would soon sail out for overseas assignment.

Three days later and two thousand men strong, the replacement group boarded the *Bloemfontein,* an old Dutch ship that functioned as our transport. We questioned how it had made the trip from Holland, and, more appropriately, whether it would be able to take us to wherever we were going. For certain, it was not the *Queen Mary.*

The entire crew was Dutch. The announcements on the public address system were made in Dutch, which gave us reason to wonder if we had boarded the right troopship. Someone remarked, "Are we sure we're not on a POW ship taking us to Germany?" The crew, however, did play some of our songs—their entire repertoire of about twelve records—all day long, over and over, for the entire journey.

We reached Hawaii, where we were to rendezvous with others to form a convoy for the remainder of the trip. We docked for several days as other vessels entered the harbor. After a few days, we were notified that the convoy would leave the next morning. But when we awoke, we were amazed to find that the *Bloemfontein* was the only ship in the harbor. The convoy had left without us! Because we were the slowest ship, and the convoy could not travel faster than the slowest ship, we would have put the convoy at a great risk.

We did leave the following morning, however, with the protection of a destroyer escort that remained with us for a few days. The remainder of the trip was made without an escort. We were on our own. We stopped at the Marshall Islands for refueling and to take on supplies.

During the entire trip we were given two meals, one at 1000 (10:00 A.M.) and the other at 1600 (4:00 P.M.). We washed and showered with filtered seawater, which always left a residue of salt on our bodies. Fresh water was reserved for cooking and drinking. We held boxing matches every evening on deck. Angelo "Bert" Bertelli was the match-maker, Doug Boyd and I worked the corners. Poker was a popular pastime, but there was a short supply of playing cards, so we alternated players. Every third hand, a player had to surrender his seat to a waiting participant. Thus we were able to accommodate all enthusiasts. Our daily regimen included calisthenics and weaponry training. Of course, throughout the day we were subjected to the music of Benny

Goodman, Tommy Dorsey, and Glenn Miller over and over, again and again.

One evening after supper there was an epidemic of food poisoning caused by contaminated Spanish olives. Men suffering from stomach pain and nausea rushed to sick bay for relief. Some made it to the head (toilets) to relieve themselves, others to the rail to upchuck. As one of the victims, I remember my friends, Bertelli and Boyd, visiting me in sick bay, flauntingly tempting me with food they had carried from the mess hall. They knew I would have a negative reaction to the sight and odor of food. They enjoyed their prankish exercise at my expense.

As we continued toward our destination, the crew of the *Bloemfontein* engaged in gunnery practice. For a half hour or so each day they fired their antiaircraft guns at a tow-target. We anxiously observed their practice, waiting to cheer them whenever they succeeded in their efforts. Throughout all those days, there was no cause to cheer. Realizing their ineptness, we asked our superiors to issue ammunition to us.

We finally arrived at Guam as replacements in the Third Marine Division thirty-four days after leaving San Diego. I was assigned to K Company, Third Battalion, Ninth Regiment.

Now, after training and securing Guam, our division was preparing for a new battle. During this time, I learned that an extra officer had joined our battalion. I did not see him the day he arrived, but someone from headquarters told me I knew him. As soon as I could, I went to the newcomer's tent to greet him. It was a surprise to see Lt. John "Red" Baker, a college classmate. I had not seen him since I left Bucknell University—and here we were on Guam getting ready for a new campaign. Baker didn't have much time to unpack his gear or get acquainted with the others. He told me that he had been flown from Pearl Harbor to join our division, knowing that we would soon leave for combat. He was to remain unassigned until the battalion decided during the battle which company needed him most. We got him.

On February 12, 1945, we were on the dock at the harbor on Guam loading our equipment aboard the troop ship USS *Leedstown,* which was to take us to our next campaign. We needed two medical corpsmen to bring our company up to full strength. Each platoon was assigned one corpsman, and my platoon was due to receive one. I noticed two men carrying full gear walking toward us. I assumed that they were our new assignments. One was much bigger than the other and appeared much stronger. Selfishly, I hoped he would be assigned to my platoon. Instead, I was assigned the smaller one. I wasn't too happy, since I did not think he would be able to perform as well as the other man. His performance in combat, however, would soon prove that my first impression was awfully wrong.

He was Corpsman Troy Young, from Duncanville, Texas, and he turned out to be outstanding. In the heat of combat, he kept his cool. Without regard to his own safety, he consistently exposed himself to certain death while caring for the wounded. He saved many lives. He never seemed to tire of helping us. He treated the wounded of other companies as well. He had the "battleside manner" that eased the stress of any wounded Marine. I'm glad he took care of me when I got hit because I knew I was in good hands. We all felt that way.

I was told that the big corpsman had to be evacuated to the ship on the second day because he cracked under the strain; later he returned to our unit. I now apologize to Corpsman Young for my original hasty and inconclusive evaluation of his potential value. May the Lord bless him for his great deeds of courage in serving his fellow man.

Medical corpsmen do not carry a weapon. They are not there to kill, but to minister to the wounded. The symbol of the red cross is prominently marked on the corpsman's sleeve and helmet to signify to the enemy that he is not a combatant. The symbol is intended to provide refuge and protection to the corpsman. But in the Pacific war, and especially on Iwo Jima, the corpsman was not only fair game but a prime target of the enemy.

On one occasion, Doc Young was sharing K rations with 1st Sgt. William E. Moore during a lull period when a Japanese attacked them. The man was overpowered and fell on Young, and Moore fell on the attacker. "With two of them on top of me, I couldn't move," Young remembers. "My face was shoved into the dirt and I could hardly breathe. I finally managed to get out from under. Sergeant Moore and I later laughed about it, joking he attacked us to steal our K rations. But we both realized it was a close call."

Near the end of the campaign, after caring for the wounded and saving many lives, Young himself was wounded. He remains a glowing memory to those of us who witnessed his valor, disregarding his own personal safety.

Chapter 2

En Route

A t dawn on St. Valentine's Day 1945, the Third Marine Division set sail on the USS *Leedstown* from its training base on Guam for an unknown destination—unknown to all except our military leaders and the Japanese-controlled radio network disc jockey, Tokyo Rose. While en route, we learned that our destination was Iwo Jima, a small island strategically located halfway between Guam in the Mariana Islands and Tokyo. The Fourth and Fifth Divisions already under way were the assault forces. Our division, the Third, was the floating reserve, to land if needed.

While awaiting our destiny, our time was spent attending briefing sessions and studying the huge relief map of the island. We were told that the island had been pounded heavily from the air and sea. For seventy-four days prior to our D-day, our bombers returning from their mission to the Japanese homeland had dropped their unexpended bombs on Iwo. The navy's task force shelled the island for three

Lt. (jg) Josh Burns, *right,* and I had known one another back home in Jersey City but met by chance on the troop transport, USS *Leedstown.* On February 14, 1945, the *Leedstown* left Guam for Iwo Jima. Over sixty thousand Marines fought for thirty-four days, followed by two days of unorganized skirmishes, on this tiny island one-third the size of Manhattan.

days prior to our landing. 16-inch shells (the navy's most powerful at that time) from seven battleships traversed Iwo back and forth continuously. Cruisers and destroyers fired upon selected targets.

K Company's executive officer, Lt. Clyde McGinnis, Lt. Raymond Ickes, and I discussed the impending possibilities of the campaign. The United States had attained naval and air superiority and had succeeded in cutting the enemy's supply line. Our intelligence reports indicated a short but hard campaign, and we paid little attention to Tokyo Rose when we heard her tell us, en route to Iwo, that after the fighting our division would be able to assemble in a telephone booth.

Since we were the division in reserve, and in view of the heavy preinvasion shelling of the island, we wondered if we would be required to land. I remarked that it would be disappointing to have come all that distance and not be called upon in the campaign. Lieutenant McGinnis contended that the losses would be heavy. We made a friendly wager of a bottle of brandy based on whether or not we would land. Lieutenant Ickes just listened, although I am sure he had his thoughts on the matter. I added that I would be embarrassed and unable to face our friends if we did not land. McGinnis replied, "Brother, if we land, there won't be enough friends left for you to face."

I then thought of the helpless feeling those poor Japanese must have had on that island. Taking a severe aerial and naval bombardment for that long period of time—with the accompanying noise and concussion—either should have killed them or driven them out of their minds. They had been notified by the Japanese high command that no help would be forthcoming. They must have known they were doomed because there was no way of escape, except to completely repel our attack. In spite of the heavy and sustained bombardment prior to landing, very few of the enemy had been killed. At the time I was not aware of their underground facilities that had protected them from our aerial and naval attacks.

The rest of the division also speculated about what to expect. Some bragged about past campaigns and some played cards to occupy the time. We were fed steaks, eggs, milk, and much of what was missing from our normal rations. One Marine became seasick on the third day and ran to the rail, heaving some of that good food along with his dentures. His buddies joked unceasingly about his dilemma. He replied, "As soon as this battle is over and we get back to Guam, I'm going to write to my dentist back in the States for a duplicate set." He didn't. As I remember, he was killed soon after we landed.

Iwo Jima, a tiny dot on the map some three thousand miles west of Hawaii and seven hundred miles south of Japan, is the remnant of an erupted volcano that popped out of the ocean. The island, whose name means Sulfur Island for its numerous underground sulfur springs, is four and a half miles long, two and a half miles at its widest point, a half mile at its narrowest, and only eight square miles in area. At its southernmost tip stands Mt. Suribachi, with a slope of approximately 45 degrees ascending to its summit nearly 560 feet above sea level. The southern portion of the island is covered with volcanic ash (black sand), making footing or traction extremely difficult. Except for a stretch of a few hundred yards of the beach, the island is protected by natural barriers, impregnable offshore rocks, and a strong, treacherous undertow. Rugged terrain and cliffs dominate the northern end. This ashen, forsaken island became a costly piece of real estate in the Pacific Ocean during World War II.

Iwo Jima was first chartered by the Spanish in 1543. It was visited by the English in 1673 and the Russians in 1805. In 1823, it was claimed by an American whaler captain; thirty years later Commo. Matthew Perry sought to erect the American flag to claim the island for the United States. Congress refused both proposals. Finally, without objection from other nations, Japan established formal claim in 1861, using the island to produce sulfur and sugar cane. In 1937, "No Trespassing" signs were posted to ward off all outsiders; then a formidable, fortified stronghold was secretly developed that would become a key element in protecting this gateway to Tokyo.

Emperor Hirohito and his chief advisor, War Lord Hideki Tojo, considered Iwo Jima the one bastion Japan could not afford to lose. On a direct line between Tokyo and our superfortress bases in Saipan in the Marianas, Iwo was the outpost for the mainland. Its position allowed the Japanese who were stationed there to alert Tokyo of our oncoming bomber raids, thus eliminating the element of surprise, and gave them a base for their fighter planes to intercept our bombers en route to Japan. Their control of the island also negated any possibility of landing our bombers that were low on fuel or disabled on their return trip to Saipan. For these reasons it was imperative that we eradicate the enemy's advantages. Moreover, the taking of Iwo would enable our fighter planes to escort the superfortresses on their missions to their mainland.

It was as important for Japan to hold Iwo Jima as it was for us to take it. Consequently, Tojo assigned Lt. Gen. Tadamichi Kuribayashi, one of Japan's best military minds, the dubious honor of defending the rock. The general spoke English and was well acquainted with American methods of operation. During the 1920s, he had served as a military envoy in Washington, D.C., and at the Fort Bliss Cavalry School, Texas.

Lieutenant General Kuribayashi was a taskmaster and lost no time in strengthening manpower and equipment on Iwo. He quickly devised plans and personally supervised the construction of three airfields and developed sixteen miles of connected underground tunnels from one end of the island to the other. The tunnels also served as living quarters for twenty-one thousand of Japan's best-trained Imperial Guard Division, who had vowed to defend the island to the last man. Kuribayashi also built a network of 1,500 interconnecting, honeycomb-like caves in the northern end of the island. The only accessible landing area was a short strip of beach at the foot of Mt. Suribachi, whose nearly 560 feet provided the Japanese with a perfect vantage point. It became an observation post as well as a fortress, with gun emplacements zeroed in on the landing strip and capable of hitting any inch of the island.

This was the scenario for the Third, Fourth, and Fifth Marine Divisions, sixty thousand strong, who were destined for an unprecedented critical rendezvous with the Japanese Imperial forces.

Part 2

Landing

Chapter 3

On the Alert

At 1000 (10:00 A.M.) on February 19, 1945, the USS *Leedstown* arrived at Iwo Jima. The Fourth and Fifth Marine Divisions had landed almost two hours earlier, at 0800. The ship's public address system announced that the assault elements of the Fourth and Fifth Divisions had met with light resistance. For a while we thought that the preinvasion bombardment had been effective and we feared it would not be necessary for us to land.

Later reports indicated that the divisions had encountered extreme shelling and continuous firing from mortars, machine guns, rockets, and rifles, while subsequent reports revealed that they had suffered heavy losses. American casualties were running high with only little progress. The Japanese allowed the early waves of Marines to come ashore relatively unhindered. When enough of them advanced into an open area without any semblance of protection, the enemy opened fire. Because the Japanese fired from hidden locations and used smokeless powder in their ammunition, their positions could not be detected. Our men were as vulnerable as sitting ducks in a shooting gallery. The soft volcanic ash hampered firm footing, slowing down our movement. Unable to attain necessary traction, our motorized equipment was stalled to a halt. As a result, the phantom, vicious, stubborn enemy forces inflicted heavy losses. Our regiment, the Ninth Marines, was notified to prepare to disembark several times, only to be delayed because the cluttered beach made landing virtually impossible. Thus we remained on the alert, waiting until the beach was cleared of the disabled tanks and halftracks. It seemed to us that we would never land.

This postfighting photograph of the landing beaches on the southern end of the island shows the terrain over which the Third, Fourth, and Fifth Marine Divisions advanced in full view of heavily fortified enemy gun emplacements. In the distance, looming over the southernmost tip of the island, is Mt. Suribachi, whose height of nearly 560 feet provided a natural observation point. Until it was taken by the Twenty-eighth Marine Regiment, the Japanese could fire from there onto any position we had established or were pursuing.

The coarse volcanic terrain made our movement forward slow and laborious. The volcanic ash hampered our footing, the high angle of the slope limited our firing view during the initial landings, and our tanks were unable to gain traction in the black sand. Our progress was measured by inches as we struggled to advance.

In the meantime the Marines of the Twenty-eighth Regiment, Fifth Division, suffered heavy losses in their assault to cut off Mt. Suribachi from the rest of the island. They succeeded in their objective by taking control at the narrowest strip of the island.

At dawn on February 22, Lt. Harold G. Schrier led the ascent to the top of Mt. Suribachi, surprisingly with light opposition. Upon reaching the summit at 1000 (10:00 A.M.), he and some of his patrol raised our flag tied to the end of an iron pipe. The flag was later replaced by a larger flag to enable all to see that we had control of the highest point of the island. Joe Rosenthal, a photographer for the Associated Press, snapped the photo, which became the most popular symbol of our victory. The flag was visible to all points of the island as well as to the ships in the bay. Horns from our ships blasted continuously to acknowledge the feat. When we on the USS *Leedstown* saw our flag waving majestically over Mt. Suribachi,

Associated Press photographer Joe Rosenthal captured this image of the second flag raising on Mt. Suribachi. The Pulitzer Prize–winning photograph was the most popular symbol of the U.S. victory on Iwo Jima and of U.S. heroism during the Pacific war.

we erupted in a spontaneous cheer that was probably heard miles away. When we finally settled down, we were overcome with a strong urge to get ashore—before it was all over.

While we waited we also witnessed our fighter planes strafing enemy positions. The area was filled with aerial activity. One of our planes was shot down, followed by a streak of smoke into the ocean. A destroyer rushed to the scene in an attempt to save the pilot, but to no avail. Ships of all sizes and categories were in close proximity to each other. I saw our cruiser hit one of our own transport ships, literally knocking the paint off its side. While this was interesting to us as observers, we preferred the role of participants and anxiously waited the call. To be returned to our base in Guam was unacceptable. Our impatience was prevalent throughout the unit. Let's go!

Bill Madden

Pvt. Bill Madden, of Bradenton, Florida, was in E Company, Twenty-seventh Marine Regiment. He was among the first to hit the beach on D-day. He recalls the thundering shells from our battleships rocking his landing craft while an antiaircraft gun downed one of our planes into the sea.

Madden remembers rushing onto the beach in the midst of shelling from enemy artillery and mortar emplacements. Their unseen machine gun and rifle positions allowed the Japanese to pick off individual targets. "Twenty-five percent of our first wave and twenty percent of the second wave were killed or wounded in the first two hours of the attack," he recalls.

Madden decided to change his foxhole to another one twenty-five feet away. The next morning he realized that the foxhole he had vacated had become a crater as a result of a direct artillery hit.

The three days it took to take Mt. Suribachi lessened the threat of being hit from the rear by enemy fire. Madden recalls, "Taking Suribachi was a relief, but the worst fighting was still to come in capturing the airfields and cleaning out the caves in the northern cliffs where the retreating enemy had reorganized. . . . Forever impressed on my mind are the sights and sounds of young boys being ripped apart by the steel fragments of mortar shells. I will never forget the unmistakable *ka-zoon* of mortar shells exploding into a clustered body of troops and the *zing* of

The cluttered beach delayed the landing of the Third Marine Division. On February 23, the fifth day of the battle, we received the order to land and begin the mission to secure the center of the island, the strongest point of the Japanese defense. We encountered the most heavily fortified portion of the island at Motoyama Airfield No. 2. Movement forward was met by heavy enemy resistance and was extremely slow. Concealed enemy positions led to high Marine casualties.

fragments of sand and steel flying past my ears as I dived for cover."

Of the 252 officers and enlisted men in E Company, only 12 came through unscathed.

James Wallover

1st Lt. James Wallover, of Beaver, Pennsylvania, landed on D-day as an artillery forward observer attached to the Twenty-fourth Regiment.

He relates the extreme difficulty getting the 105-mm howitzers ashore and setting up their positions. "In the first few days there was little forward movement with many casualties. The heavy guns were virtually ineffective in the early phases. We had to rely on naval gunfire for infantry support."

On D plus three, he moved ahead looking for a suitable location to establish a new position. He remembers going out some fifty yards in dead silence. "It was an uneasy sensation. There must have been many eyes on my crew as we moved about, but not a single shot. We could feel their presence but could not see them in their heavily fortified protection. We moved back to our original location and I can't imagine why they didn't open fire. It took a few days for the troops to advance to that same spot because of strong resistance. I guess they didn't consider my crew an important target or they waited for more of us to get into their sights.

"On about February 25, our team was in a shell hole near Meat Grinder Hill. A mortar shell landed in the same hole. There were several wounded, including the rifle company captain, who had his leg blown off. Paul Maloff, from Syracuse, one of my team, tied a tourniquet to stop the bleeding while we waited for the medical corpsman. I learned later that the captain had played half-back for the New York Giants."

One morning early in March as he moved forward, Wallover saw a Japanese rise up out of the rocks and shoot at him. A sterling silver chain, a gift from his wife, and his dog tags were hit and he was knocked down. When the man rose to fire again, Wallover got him. He said, "It was his last move; he was dead."

A few days later, Wallover's men advanced to a large mound from which he could direct fire. "It was near dusk when I noticed Japs moving in on us from both sides and from our front. The infantry had apparently pulled back for the night. I was hit in the face and arms with a grenade. I called back to our battery for fire to cover our withdrawal. We ran as the 105-mm rounds hit the mound just as the Japs had reached it. We made it back.

"On March 8, the Japs used an unusual device, a missile or rocket that looked like a flying bucket, the size of a five-gallon bucket with a three-foot-long pipe and fins. They would explode before hitting the ground and spray metal fragments in all directions. They were intended to inflict injury on personnel rather than equipment. They made a weird characteristic sound as they moved slowly through the air. We could tell when they were coming, giving us time to take whatever cover was available. They might have looked crude, but they did cause many casualties."

Wallover became one of these casualties. He was hit in the back and hip. He was flown back to Guam, then Hawaii to recover. He eventually was reassigned to active duty as the war came to an end. He states, "We knew then that all six Marine divisions were destined to land in the initial attack on the Japanese homeland. We would have been slaughtered. Thank God for the atomic bomb."

Chapter 4

Over the Side

On February 23, the day after the flag raising at Mt. Suribachi, we finally received the order to disembark. This time the order was not rescinded. Bill Crawford, our captain, explained our plan: we were to gather at the edge of Motoyama Airfield No. 1, one of three airfields on the island, and await further instruction.

We went over the side and into the landing crafts heading toward the beach. Our crafts were tossed by the big waves and swift undertow. As we approached the beach, Mt. Suribachi in its majestic size looked down on us and appeared to beckon us sinisterly to land. Its height of nearly 560 feet cannot be appreciated unless it is expressed in terms of something to which one can relate: it is as high as the Washington Monument or, according to architectural standards, as tall as a forty-four-story office building.

I gazed at the others in the craft; their faces reflected the appearance of purpose, determination, seriousness, and an occasional smile. There was a definite air of exhilaration among the men. Morale was high and contagious. The feeling can be best described as that of an impatient football player sitting on the bench and eagerly waiting to be called by the coach to get into the game. Our anxiety to "get into the game" supplanted any sense of fear. Yes, certainly there was apprehension about not knowing what to expect, but there definitely was not fear at this point—that came later. Approaching the island, we were overcome by the purpose of our mission and dedicated to achieving the expected high level of our performance.

After the Fourth and Fifth Divisions had secured a toehold on the beach, the Fifth swung left to Mt. Suribachi and to the west shore while the Fourth turned north along the east coast. Elements of both divisions advanced inward on Airfield No. 1, just a few hundred yards from the beach.

Airfield No. 1 was located in the southern part of Iwo Jima where the island is just about one mile wide. The flat terrain offered no protection from the invisible enemy firing from undetected positions. That, coupled with the congestion of men in a condensed area in a frontal attack, resulted in a heavy loss of lives. It was at this point in time that the Twenty-first and Ninth Regiments of the Third Division were called to spearhead the center of the line and pursue the attack on Airfield No. 2. The Third Regiment of the Third Division remained afloat in reserve.

When we reached the beach, the ramp was lowered. We rushed out and, in compliance with Captain Crawford's orders, ran up to the designated location, the edge of Airfield No. 1.

As soon as we regrouped, Lieutenant McGinnis told me to follow him to a certain large shell crater, which he had selected as an observation post for K Company and from which I could direct my mortar fire. We reached it only to be greeted by enemy shells. McGinnis turned to me and said, "Damn, this is a hot place." In that crater with us was the body of a Marine who had just been killed. He was sitting against the slope of the crater, a cigarette still burning between two of his fingers and a rifle in his other hand. He had been decapitated.

Having met our first objective, to pass through another company that had been pinned down between Airfield No. 1 and Airfield No. 2, we moved on toward our next objective, to capture Motoyama Airfield No. 2. As we approached the airfield, I was pinned down by enemy machine gunfire. The bullets peppered the ground all around me, coming close enough to kick the dirt onto my face. It stung so hard I thought I had been hit. I brushed my hands across my face and reluctantly pulled them down, expecting to see blood. Seeing none, I moved out of there fast and joined McGinnis. Having witnessed it all he asked, "Now are you glad you landed?"

Clyde "Mac" McGinnis

The most understanding and congenial person in our company was Lt. Clyde McGinnis, from Tulsa, Oklahoma. He was about thirty years of age, which was the basis for his claim as the oldest man in K Company. McGinnis was a former track star at Oklahoma University and had run against the legendary Glenn Cunningham in college. His proudest possession was a photo of his wife and his two little girls. I think every man in the outfit had seen the picture of his family. It gave all of us a sense of pride to know our executive officer had a charming wife and two beautiful kids.

If any single individual could be credited for the high spirit and morale of K Company, it would be Lieutenant McGinnis. His cheerfulness and wit, under the most adverse situations, were unparalleled. He had the capacity to ease a tense situation with a timely remark. I was always comfortable going to him for advice.

If any single individual could be credited for the high spirit and morale of K Company, it would be Lieutenant McGinnis. Always with a smile and ready to help anyone, the "old sage" was really too good to be exposed to the enemy. I used to kid him that the Marine Corps would keep him in the war longer than anyone else, and that by the time he did get home, his daughters would be grown up and his wife wouldn't recognize him. Courtesy of Jan McGinnis Kaye

McGinnis had been through two campaigns when I met him, a master of the finesse of warfare. Some of the little things I learned on Guam and Iwo Jima came as a result of his tutelage. Always with a smile and ready to help anyone, the "old sage" was really too good to be exposed to the enemy. I used to kid him that the Marine Corps would keep him in the war longer than anyone else, and that by the time he did get home, his daughters would be grown up and his wife wouldn't recognize him.

Once when we were under the heaviest of artillery and mortar barrage, McGinnis jumped into my foxhole, looked at me, smiled, and began singing the first lines of "Take Me Back to Tulsa." After a time, he decided to return to the company command post and told me to wait in the foxhole. He threw off his pack and took off running and jumping a step or two ahead of enemy fire. Approximately half an hour later I saw him heading back, dodging bullets in the same manner. He yelled jokingly from a distance, "I'll be right there, but I do think those guys are trying to kill me." A moment later he was hit by shrapnel, injuring both of his legs, his arms, and his chest. He was unconscious when the medical corpsman placed him on the stretcher to be carried back to the battalion aid station.

The next time I saw Lieutenant McGinnis was in the hospital at Pearl Harbor one month later. Both of us were on crutches. As we looked at each other and laughed, I demanded payment of our wager. A few days later he was returned to the States. When he was about to leave, he smiled and asked, his eyes sparkling, "Do you think my wife and daughters will recognize the old man now?"

Burt "Red" Doran

Cpl. Burt "Red" Doran, of Boone, Iowa, was an experienced Browning automatic rifleman and a "gung-ho" Marine. He was soft spoken and performed his job well. While training for Iwo Jima on Guam, we established competition with other companies in basketball and softball during periods of recreation. Doran was an excellent athlete; he played hard and played to win. That quality carried over into combat as he fought for his country.

Doran was severely wounded early in the battle. Later at the hospital in Hawaii, I noticed that he was blind. I extended my sympathies and offered some words of encouragement. Doran was not one to feel sorry for himself, and he did not want anyone else to feel sorry for him. He accepted his fate and preferred to talk about the rest of the men in the company. He asked what had happened to them and to me. He showed more concern for those who were more fortunate in their injuries than he was in his. We concluded our conversation when we were told that it was time to eat lunch. Two of Doran's friends from another unit, also blind, came over to us. Doran introduced me to them and asked me to have chow with them. I was honored to join them. As we walked through the hospital corridor on the way to the mess hall Doran and his two buddies broke out in song, chanting "Three Blind Mice."

Chapter 5

Lieutenant, You're in Charge

Motoyama Airfield No. 2 was a ridge several hundred yards of open terrain to our front. The attack hour was 1600 (4:00 P.M.) on February 24. We advanced well against light opposition, which brought us to an open, flat area void of any defilade except for shell craters. As soon as we had advanced far enough so that we could not get out, the enemy fire started. The fire from artillery, mortars, machine guns, and rifles at once threatened to smother us. One would swear that all the gates of hell had opened simultaneously. Everything from all sides focused on us. That was the enemy's mode of operation—to allow us to advance into an open area without cover and then open fire.

Until we could get our own artillery to counter fire, we were helpless. Our only refuge was to hug the dirt, get behind a few small rocks or a little crater in the ground, hope, pray, and sweat it out. I found myself too far in front of the rest of the company. Enemy shells broke my phone wires and there was too much enemy fire to send my runner back.

Consequently, I lost contact with the rest of the company. All I could see when I turned to look back were men—men being hit, men running for cover. We eventually jumped into a large shell crater. Because I did not know the exact location of K Company's command post, I had to wait until the barrage let up a bit before attempting to contact it. The barrage refused to subside, however, and I received no sign or word from the command post or the other units. We had gone too far and were isolated from the others. We made a few attempts to get back, only to learn that the enemy still knew where we were and had hit the first two men I sent to make it back. We had never been in a situation like this. The Japanese could see us and were hitting us, but we could not see them or determine from where they were firing. They seemed to be invisible.

It was a seriously sobering experience to realize that all eyes in my platoon were turned toward me, their lieutenant. We were trapped by the enemy and cut off from the rest of the company. Any move we made was answered by snipers' bullets. I knew that if we remained there too long we wouldn't have a chance to get out. The men didn't have to say it. The look on their faces revealed their feelings. I was the officer and it was up to me to get us out of there. The impact of my decision, whatever it would be, began to weigh heavily on my mind. I was dealing with lives of men, and this was not a training exercise. It was the real thing and my first big test, on my own.

It was not yet dark, so to send more men out while the enemy could still see us would be futile; yet if we waited for darkness, they would surely attack. Therefore, as soon as it got dark we began to crawl on our bellies, one at a time, to rejoin our company. We made it back in several hours, suffering two casualties.

Strangely, I could not locate any of the other officers of K Company. I then crawled to Lt. "Moose" Scanlon of I Company, who confirmed the distressing news that Capt. Bill Crawford had been killed. I managed to get back to Sgt. Bill Moore, who reported that about 70 of the 230 men of the company had been hit in those few hours of slaughter. When we landed I was sixth in seniority among the seven officers of K Company. Now, all in that brief span, Sergeant Moore informed me, "Lieutenant, you're in charge of K Company." Then, casually, he added apologetically, "Lieutenant, I had to report you missing in action. I didn't know what happened to you and the platoon."

Death struck swiftly for both U.S. and Japanese soldiers. In the first few hours after landing, about 70 of the 230 men in K Company—including six of its seven officers—had been killed or wounded. Casualties were high throughout the campaign: over six thousand Marines were killed in action. Following Japan's "no reinforcements" and "no surrender" strategy, nearly all of the estimated twenty-one thousand highly trained Japanese Imperial Guard stationed on the island perished.

We reorganized what was left of our company and prepared to hold our line against possible counterattack. Enemy shells kept dropping on us all night long. We received a few moments of rest only when the enemy got tired of firing at us. My thoughts kept gravitating to the captain and the others who had been hit. I never thought that the Japanese could manufacture a bullet capable of killing Bill Crawford. Without him I knew only too well that the rest of the campaign was going to be the worst we had ever seen.

A few days later, we recaptured the area where my platoon had been cut off from the rest of the company. I learned why we were being hit without knowing where the enemy was: the Japanese were shooting at us from two of our own disabled tanks that had been abandoned just thirty or forty yards away. I never imagined that they would crawl into our own tanks to shoot at us. That was the last place I expected them to be.

Bill Crawford

The most remarkable man I have ever seen in combat was Capt. Bill Crawford, from Calvin, North Dakota. He was in his middle twenties, indestructible, rough, rugged, and ready for combat at anytime. As a leader of men, he had no equal. As rifle company officers under him, we were always conscious of placing the men first. Captain Crawford made certain that the enlisted men ate before the officers and that they were dug in their foxholes before the officers started to dig theirs. He constantly reminded us that "war is the most serious business at hand" and that as officers "we are charged with the responsibility to protect the lives of our men. Don't ever forget that!" He demanded much of all of us in the company and we would follow him wherever he was ready to lead.

Captain Crawford had been in command of K Company through Bougainville and Guam. Just before embarking for Iwo Jima, he had qualified for thirty days' leave back home, but had rejected his turn of rotation just to be with us for the next operation. Together, we went through rigorous training on Guam. The captain was too much a part of K Company to allow anyone else to lead us into combat. I remember him saying, "I'll go home after this one."

All the confidence and respect that we saw in Bill Crawford accompanied us when we landed. With him we were ready for anything the enemy had to offer. On the first day, having met our immediate objective, Captain Crawford ordered us to press on.

That was the last time I saw him alive. I learned from Pvt. Ishmael Gonzalez, of Chicago, the captain's wireman and runner, that Crawford was hit while charging ahead, shouting orders to one of the platoon leaders who had strayed slightly off course. His runner told me that he had been shot through the head. A corpsman tried to help him, but he refused the aid. Against his wishes, they pulled him behind a rock for protection. He ordered them to let him alone and to take care of the others who were hit. He died behind that rock.

A few days later when they removed the dead, the body that had housed the indestructible, courageous, and aggressive Bill Crawford was now lifeless. From my foxhole I saw his arms dangling over the side of the stretcher as the litter carriers ran off with his body—a most unexpected and stirring scene. I thought of the pictures of his family he had proudly displayed. Then I remembered how he used to talk about remaining in the Marine Corps after the war was over. Crawford did not live to remain in the Marine Corps, but his name did; it always will. The athletic field and parade grounds where we had spent many hours while stationed on Guam were named in his honor.

Chapter 6

Motoyama Airfield No. 2

Taking Airfield No. 2 had seemed unattainable and had proved very costly to us. We did not gain appreciable ground for two days. The enemy overpowered us with constant shelling. Whenever we attempted to move over that wide, flat terrain we became easy targets. The airstrip had offered no concealment or defilade except for shell craters. If we managed to get into one, the Japanese knew we were there and waited patiently for us to pop out. Their patience outlasted our anxiety.

It was evident: we had confronted the impossible mission. We were on the southeastern bank of the mile-wide airstrip, which provided some protection from direct rifle and machine gun fire, but not from the overhead mortar and artillery shells. As we attempted to take the runway we were forced back time and again.

Even under the cover of mortar and artillery fire, we had lost many men, yet accounted for very little yardage. Replacements coming up to us were hit as they reached the open area behind us. If we tried to go back for ammunition, we were picked off. The enemy could see us, but we could not see them. Stalled in our tracks and failing in attempt after attempt, we were at the point of no return. I had wondered if we would ever take this barren strip.

I was certain all of us realized the precarious position, though none revealed it. As an officer I had to portray a positive and confident air, although my personal, hidden fear was that the Japanese were capable of mustering a massive attack to completely destroy us or drive us back to the sea.

We could not outflank them; a frontal assault had been the only approach, and the enemy was well aware of that. To make matters worse, we had had to surmount the two-hundred-foot terrace at the edge of the airfield. Unable to gain traction, our tanks had been useless. I had requested naval gunfire support from the destroyer assigned to our battalion. The ship's forward observer who accompanied us ordered the support. Some of the shells had fallen among our position. I immediately fired a red flare to cease fire. Corrections were made and the destroyer resumed the shelling. It did not seem to make much difference. As soon as our firing stopped, the enemy responded with theirs, almost as a gesture of defiance. I felt that if we let them fire all they want, perhaps they would run out of ammunition.

I had wondered, what would it require for us to take the airfield? We were losing men and not gaining any ground. Was this to become a blemish on the tradition of the Marine Corps? Would the enemy counterattack and push us back to the beach? We would then have to retake all that land. We could not allow that to happen. That would be an awful chapter in the annals of the Marine Corps, a disgraceful episode in our proud history. But more important than the dignity and pride of the Corps was the concern for the lives of the men.

Even if we could not advance, we at least had to hold our position. I had informed our colonel, Harold Boehm, of our status and had requested more replacements and concerted support of heavy artillery, naval, and aerial firepower to weaken the enemy's positions—wherever they were.

Col. Harold Boehm, commander of the Third Battalion, Ninth Regiment, came up to the front on that third day to personally assess the situation. I saw him jumping from one shell hole to the other, dodging shelling and sniper bullets. As the lone surviving officer I briefed him on our predicament and pointed to where I thought the enemy's heavy fire positions were located. Only an all-out effort by our forces could ensure our advance, I added. Colonel Boehm offered words of encouragement and praised our resolve. He assured us of more replacements and naval and aerial support for our next assault. He kidded the men about the good meals being served aboard ship that night, then, turning to his runner, jokingly said, "Now we have to get back. You go first to see if they're shooting at us." The bewildered look on the runner's face revealed that he wasn't sure if the colonel was serious.

Our level of morale was lifted by Colonel Boehm's presence in our lines. He understood our dilemma and showed his concern by risking his neck. He demonstrated that he was a man of men, one of us.

Upon his return to the command post, Colonel Boehm ordered a sustained naval, aerial, and artillery shelling on the probable enemy emplacements, which was coordinated with our assault. With reserve support and the aerial and naval bombardment, we eventually succeeded in crossing the airfield. At the other side of the airstrip, we saw the enemy and were subjected to uninterrupted small arms fire and the loss of more men. Exchanging gunfire, we were able to drive the enemy back. The image of the Marine Corps had remained

intact and our spirit and confidence had been restored, sufficient to energize our continued forward advance.

Bill Bryant

Cpl. Bill Bryant, of Louisville, Kentucky, was a journeyman
machine gunner, a veteran of the Bougainville and Guam
campaigns. He was wounded after a couple of days on Iwo.
He stated, "Iwo was the worst. A few days on Iwo are capable of a lifetime of haunting memories.

K Company Machine Gunner Cpl. Bill Bryant: "Iwo was the worst.
A few days on Iwo are capable of [making] a lifetime of haunting
memories." Courtesy of Bill Bryant

"When we went ashore it looked like black sand, but it was volcanic ash—two steps forward and one step back all the way." He remembers, "On the beach I saw dead bodies lying about. We spent the night at the base of Airfield No. 2. Mortars and artillery shells rained over us all night long. They had buzz-booms that sounded like a freight train—the first we had heard about or seen buzz-booms.

"The next day we advanced onto the airfield against light resistance. We joined with two battalions of the Twenty-first Marines, also of the Third Marine Division. Three of our tanks came along in formation when our K Company captain, Bill Crawford, told me to keep an eye on the antiaircraft guns on the hill in front of us. I told him there weren't any Japs near the gun, then some did appear from a cave that had a steel door cover. The captain left for another part of the line. All of a sudden all hell broke loose. Many of K Company were hit. Capt. Bill Crawford was killed and I saw him fall across Vernon Huckaby's machine gun.

"Enemy mortars, larger than we had ever seen, knocked out our three tanks and hit K Company lines. It looked like half of our numbers were hit. I had a piece of shrapnel go through my pack; I tried to reach it to pull it out, but I couldn't. I asked my number one gunner, David Guess, to reach down my back and pull it out and he did. I had a large burn and still do. A jagged piece of shrapnel stuck in my back about three inches down from my shoulder near the spine, but I was still on my feet and going. Shortly after, I felt something hit my helmet. I moved my head to the side. After another blast, I reached up and realized it was Joe Haas's brains that had hit my helmet. He was some forty or fifty feet from me. Joe, also, was a machine gunner.

"I went over to help the wounded and the first person I saw was Jim Boman. He had been wounded and was holding his intestines with his left hand and arm while helping his people who had been wounded. I said that he should go to the corpsman, but his reply was, 'Not until I get all my wounded out of here.'

"It was mass destruction—wounded and dead all over. I found Dick Schriber, a machine gun section leader, still alive, but with his left kidney blown out. I asked for help to get him back to the first aid station. After getting him to the station, I came back. A day or two later, a blast took me out. I woke up on a hospital ship, some two or three days later, I am told. I was taken back to the Guam hospital and shipped home.

"I want to say that all men of K Company were affected by this campaign, even those who were not wounded. Anybody who says this wasn't frightening isn't being truthful. We all are still affected, maybe not physically, but in our minds. The memories haunt us."

Bill Bryant's granddaughter, Melissa Peak, sent me the following letter.

Dear Mr. Caruso,

The families of the men returning from war were affected by their heroes' experiences. Two generations of Bill Bryant's progeny are available to share their five decades of life in the aftermath, if you are interested. It has just been in the last five to ten years that my grandfather has begun to release the fear of his experiences. We have all lived with the symptoms of his fears, but we are just realizing how deep his psychological and emotional scars have been, how strong his psychological defense mechanisms have been, and how his behaviors were affected by the hell of war. He remains *semper fi.*

John "Red" Baker

When our company lost five of its officers on that first attack, Lt. John "Red" Baker, of Syracuse, New York, was sent as a replacement officer. He was assigned a platoon next to mine, and we had plenty of opportunity to work closely. I remember one occasion when we were getting ready to move into an attack. The word was passed along the line to find out if all platoons were ready. Baker then informed me that during the night a Japanese machine gun crew had moved in front of his sector. We knew we would eventually run into many others, but we didn't know where they would be. Here at least we knew the location of this one, which would have had the advantage of flanking fire on Baker's platoon, so he asked me to hold the attack until he had had a chance to eliminate the Japanese Nambu. I relayed the word to Colonel Boehm. I then saw Baker go out alone while his men covered his approach to the enemy position. Although he was fired upon, he managed to get near enough to throw some grenades and fire some shots from his rifle, killing the Japanese. He came back and nonchalantly said, "Okay, Pat! Tell the Colonel we're ready to go." He did all this as casually as if he were going to the corner store for a loaf of bread.

After eight days on the line and in the assault, our battalion was finally relieved. We went back to rest near the base of Mt. Suribachi. We ate ten-in-one rations, drank juice and hot coffee, and received some mail. We had to burn the mail as soon as we read it for security reasons, in the event of capture by the enemy. We looked forward to a break from the fighting that day and that night. However, before dark we were ordered back on the line in support of another battalion that had suffered heavy losses and needed our help. As we moved toward the front line again, I noticed a despondent expression on Baker's face. His eyes were tearing as he stared expressionless into space. He said nothing to me as we walked together. To draw a conversation, I began to talk about the futility of war, its waste and violence. I asked if he remembered how we worried about final exams, dating, curfew, and regulations while at Bucknell, and how useless it was to consume our energies at that time on items so trivial compared to what we now faced on Iwo. He agreed with a faint smile. Then he reluctantly told me that he had learned from one of the letters he had just received from his mother that his twin brother had been killed in combat in Germany. I was helpless in trying to find the right thing to say, and remained silent. However, my mind brought me back to a day on Guam when I had learned from my family that my youngest brother had been shot down in an aerial attack over Germany, two days after his nineteenth birthday. As we moved on I thought that it was bad enough for all of us to go back on the line again so soon, but for Baker it was going to be a greater burden.

A week or so later I was wounded. As I lay on the stretcher near the company command post, the men began to dig foxholes for the night. Baker came over to me and talked awhile, trying to console me while I waited to be moved back to the battalion aid station. That was the last time I saw or spoke to my friend, John "Red" Baker.

Two weeks later, when I was in the hospital at Pearl Harbor, I learned that he had been hit in the leg by machine gun fire. Our medical corpsman, Doc Young, took care of him and told him to rest against a rock while they were waiting for a stretcher. Baker was not one to wait. He wanted to get right back at the enemy and quickly tore off his tourniquet, grabbed his rifle, and charged the enemy position by himself. He was killed instantly—just a few days before the fighting ended.

Vernon Huckaby

Pfc. Vernon Huckaby, of Louisiana, had been a part of K Company since its early days of Bougainville and Guam before stepping foot on Iwo Jima. Vernon was a member of a machine gun crew. On the first day of our assault on Airfield No. 2, he was close enough to witness our captain, Bill Crawford, get hit. He said, "He got it right in the middle of his forehead and the bullet came out the back of his head. He never knew what hit him."

Later in the campaign Vernon was wounded by a sniper's bullet through his thigh and evacuated to Guam for recovery. "We lost too many good men there. I wouldn't take a million bucks to go through that again. They were hitting us from both sides, from the front and from the rear and we couldn't see them."

Ken Thompson

Lt. Ken Thompson, of Minnesota, had been a Spam salesman before enlisting in the Marines. We never stopped kidding him about Spam, which had become part of our regular diet.

Thompson received a field commission for his outstanding performance as a noncommissioned officer (NCO) on Bougainville and Guam. I was pleased to have him ask for the use of my gold bars for the special ceremonies making him a lieutenant. I remember he told me once that his biggest regret was that he did not marry the girl he left back home in Minnesota. While on Guam he used to send her money to put away for an engagement ring. Only a few of us knew of his prevailing pain caused by a severe case of arthritis. He rejected pity.

Of the original seven officers in our company, Thompson and I were the only two left at the end of the second day of fighting. A day or two later, we were pulled out of our line and sent to reinforce a threatened sector. We were near the north end of Airfield No. 2 when Thompson and I met with

Colonel Boehm for instructions prior to our next move. I recollect that our conversation centered on the large number of our men who had been killed. It all seemed so unbelievable. We were tired, dismayed, confused, and unable to understand why the island had not sunk into the ocean after the terrific naval bombardment and the seventy-four days of aerial attack. I distinctly remember Thompson's statement to me: "It's only a matter of which last longer, Marines or Japanese ammunitions, and it looks as though they have plenty to go." Thompson also knew that if Iwo Jima was full of diamonds and gold and only he knew about it, it would not be enough incentive to return to that island after the war. "Once I get back home to Minnesota and I marry my girl, I'll never leave."

A major, Thompson's former commanding officer, happened to pass by as we were waiting to move out and said, "Ken, I heard you were killed." Thompson smiled and said, "Sorry to disappoint you, Major, I'm still alive." The next day we were back on the line and in the assault. Later, during a Japanese counterattack, Thompson was shot through the head. The major's ill-timed remark preyed on my mind.

Part 3

Moving On

Chapter 7

Attack and Counterattack

On our sixth day ashore, we were attempting to capture a knoll north of Airfield No. 2 when we encountered heavy fire from a series of pillboxes. We took the knoll after a fight that lasted several hours, but the enemy kept dropping artillery and mortar shells on us. Colonel Boehm wanted us to hold that knoll. We lost men taking it and were going to lose more trying to hold it. The Japanese had every inch of the island zeroed in. As soon as we took one more objective, they wasted no time in shelling our newly acquired real estate.

The knoll, although only thirty to forty yards wide, was important because it gave us good forward position. The enemy was only twenty-five yards to our front, and the position gave us a commanding view of our subsequent objectives. We were at the apex of our lines, which made us vulnerable to attack. We retained possession, but by dusk there were only about twenty of us left on the line and almost all of our ammunition was expended. With darkness approaching, hope was

U.S. artillery destroying an enemy pillbox. The invading Marines fought above ground, while the defending Japanese fought below ground. The enemy's carefully constructed underground fortress—miles of inter-locking caves, concrete blockhouses, and pillboxes—was one of the most impenetrable defenses encountered by U.S. forces during the Pacific war and proved that Japan's preparations for this island were undertaken many years prior to the attack on Pearl Harbor.

fading for another unit to join us. Being up there without a unit on either side meant that we could be attacked from the front and both flanks. We couldn't even dig in because the enemy was looking down our throats all day long. I then asked the men at headquarters for more ammunition and for stretcher carriers to move out our five or six wounded. Although they couldn't spare much ammunition, they prom-ised artillery support if the enemy counterattacked. The Japanese began firing at the litter carriers as they tried to carry our wounded. We had to consume the little ammunition that was just brought to us in an attempt to cover their withdrawal. Two of the carriers were hit. What a feeling, being wounded once and knowing that they want to get you again.

We prepared ourselves for the eventual counterattack and then waited for it. Artillery shells flew over us from both directions, each side trying to hit the other's emplacements. Our telephone wires were hit constantly. My wireman spent half the night repairing them. As soon as he repaired one break, another section would be hit. It was a busy night. There was always some firing. Several times we thought the counterattack was about to materialize, but it did not. I wondered if the Japanese had miscalculated our waning numbers, if they just wanted to keep us off guard, or if perhaps they couldn't put it together. The latter might explain the reason why four small groups rushed us instead of an organized mass attack, which undoubtedly could have overwhelmed us.

Daybreak finally arrived and we welcomed it. Although it is just as painful to be hit during the day, one is spared the added complications of being hit in the darkness of night. Many men died in combat because help couldn't get to them in time during the night. I checked to see that our group was still intact and learned that the men on the left of our line had used all their ammunition against several minor counterattacks. One of my men told me that upon running out of ammunition he had rolled stones down the knoll that night, hoping the enemy would think they were hand grenades—just to keep them off balance.

A couple of hours after daybreak, the enemy started yelling and moving about. They increased their fire and began their attack. They left their emplacements just twenty-five yards to our front and charged us. Our limited supply of ammunition forced us to use what we had very carefully. I picked up my phone to call headquarters for some assistance, but our lines were broken again.

Cpl. Joe Simone, from Trenton, New Jersey, was in charge of the company's 60-mm mortars at this time. He saw what was happening and immediately directed fire from his mortars, which were placed on our slope of the knoll, to the reverse slope, where the enemy was charging us. Mortar shells are not accurate, especially at such close range, but Simone's shells fell on the charging enemy just yards to our front. Some of the shrapnel fell among us, but only a few of the enemy reached us. Corporal Simone stopped their attack. The enemy scattered back to their line when they saw what was happening. When it was all over, I counted more than sixty dead or wounded Japanese within twenty-five yards of our position. More important, we did not have a single casualty. Corporal Simone's action prevented our annihilation.

The enemy was quiet for the next few hours, and I decided to go to our command post to personally argue the need for more men and ammunition. On my way there, two Japanese antitank guns fired at me. I jumped into the nearest shell crater and was astonished to see Cpl. George Wayman there. A bazooka man, Corporal Wayman, of Elsbury, Missouri, had been in law enforcement prior to the war. He was married, the father of two children, polite, self-assured, and clean-cut. His physique and good looks caused me to imagine that he had walked right out of a Marine recruitment poster. Because of his size, Captain Crawford had assigned him to Lt. Ken Thompson's platoon to handle the bazooka, a heavy weapon designed to fire shells capable of disabling tanks and penetrating pillboxes. Corpsmen, demolitions men, and bazooka men were especially vulnerable, thus prime targets to the enemy.

By our sixth day ashore, Wayman was the only bazooka man left in K Company. Consequently, he was called upon to perform beyond the normal requirements. Such was the occasion when he had been requested to assist our platoon. While attempting to capture the knoll, he had been hit and knocked into the large shell crater where I now found him.

Wayman told me that he had been hit early the previous day. I saw he had a serious open gash in his thigh, hit by a shell that shattered his bone. He told me his corpsman was supposed to return to him the day before, but never came. Unknown to Wayman, the corpsman himself was wounded. I was the first person Wayman had seen since that previous day. He still had the pack on his back. He was completely out of water, feverish, and did not have the strength to wave the flies away from the open wound. Even if he could move out, he was in the direct line of fire of those antitank guns that had hit him and that had caused me to jump into the same crater. I was afraid that gangrene had already set in during his twenty-seven-hour ordeal of helpless waiting.

I was not a medic, but I could see that Wayman needed immediate attention. I gave him some water and promised to send help. I placed a marker on the edge of the crater and ran on to headquarters. I sent Corpsman Young and two litter carriers to Wayman; they carried him out of the fire from the heavy guns and snipers. They told me later that he would lose his leg.

After Wayman was evacuated, he spent almost two years in several hospitals, most of the time in a cast from his chest to his toes. He was eventually released to continue his life walking with a limp, bearing his battle scars and mangled leg as his badge of horror.

We lost contact with each other after Iwo. Twenty-five years later, through my Associated Press article on the anniversary of Iwo Jima, we reestablished communication. Along with some other survivors and our families we held a reunion that Wayman hosted in St. Louis. This initial meeting served as the impetus to continue our gathering on an annual basis, meeting in a different location. We alternate the responsibility of host each year.

We discuss light subject matters, such as how the volcanic black ash provided no traction and how it was so soft and light we could dig our foxhole with our hands; how you could dig a hole twelve inches deep and cook your can-ration from the embedded heat of the volcano; how to us the prevailing stench of sulfur characterized Iwo; and other discussions pertaining to dates, sequences of events, or names of our fellow Marines (as our memory fades).

There is deliberate avoidance of serious discussion of death, suffering, or killing—nothing to stimulate the memory of the mayhem. Only once in all these years has Wayman talked to me about our encounter when I jumped into the shell crater to find him severely wounded and unattended.

I recently received the following note from Wayman's daughter, Mrs. Shirley Boyles:

> Dad never said much about his war experiences to any of us. However, I do remember overhearing him make the following statement. "I was in so much pain after laying in that shell hole for so long I could hardly stand it. At times I wanted to pull my bayonet out of my pack and end my misery. Every time I started to do that, I got a mental picture of my wife and children and simply couldn't do it."

When I finally reached Colonel Boehm, he told me that my unit would be relieved within the hour. That satisfied me. I picked up a new battery to replace the dead one in my walkie-talkie and returned to the knoll. When I reached my men, I told them that we would be relieved. Our jubilation began to fade as two and then three hours passed without our replacements. Luckily, the Japanese, in the meantime, offered no trouble. I could not see them. I thought they had probably moved back to build their next line of resistance or that they were just hiding, waiting for us to pursue the attack. Whichever it was, they were quiet and out of sight and that pleased me.

We were not relieved and, for some unknown reason, the enemy was inactive for a few hours. That worried me almost as much as if they had attacked because it would soon be dark and I did not know what that night would bring. Fortunately for us, only intermittent artillery shells were falling around, but there was no sign of an enemy counterattack.

In the meantime, replacement Marines helped bolster our numbers. Replacements came on a continuous basis

A Marine digs out his rifle after being buried in his foxhole during an enemy bombardment. Historians have said the attack made by U.S. forces was like "throwing human flesh against reinforced concrete."

and near the end, the replacement Marines in K Company outnumbered the men who originally made the landing. Battle replacements were virtually assigned "by the numbers" to depleted units. Time and conditions did not allow the luxury of a formal introduction. Consequently, quite often the replacement did not know anyone in the unit and the unit did not even know the replacement's name. The situation was a difficult one because the replacements were young and inexperienced. Whereas we grew into the campaign day by day, thus becoming accustomed to the battle, they were thrust into it without proper preparation, making the situation even more difficult. They had not trained together as a unit, but had to fit in as best as they could. We hardly got to know them, their capabilities, or their weaknesses. I'm certain they felt the same about us. In the heat of the battle, however, we were all Marines.

Paul N. Ferree

Pvt. Paul N. Ferree, of Bloomington, Indiana, was a replacement assigned to K Company halfway through the campaign. Like many others, he immediately received his baptism of fire. He said the sky on his first night on Iwo was filled with tracer bullets. "It looked like a red blizzard, as though red lights were shining on falling flakes; a backdrop to a dogfight between our fighter planes and a Jap zero."

After a couple of days, his machine gun squad ran low on ammunition. He and another Marine were ordered to go back for more. They spotted an unattended stretcher on the way and used it to carry the ammunition. An officer, thinking they were stretcher carriers, ordered them to go into the ravine to carry out some of the wounded to the battalion aid station. In doing so, they were fired upon, jumped into a shell crater, waited, then continued into the throat of the enemy. In the midst of flying bullets, they managed to place the first wounded they saw onto the stretcher. As they carried him out, Ferree was shot through the hand. Although he himself was wounded, the two men continued on their mission of mercy—then Ferree was treated for his injury.

As a result of his accelerated indoctrination, Pvt. Paul Ferree, the replacement, became a battlefield journeyman in just a few days. It didn't take long to acclimate on Iwo. We were subjected to instant learning.

Robert Donahoo

Pfc. Robert Donahoo joined us as a replacement on his first day ashore during a break in the battle. I was taken by his youthful appearance, and as we advanced to the front line, I kidded him about being under age. His fresh, immaculate clothing, clean-shaven face, and innocent manner put him out of place with the rest of us who wore the dirt and stains of combat. He was obviously apprehensive, and as we walked toward the front, I tried to relax him with questions about his hometown and casual conversation.

On our way up we were hit by enemy rockets. We all jumped for cover, and when the firing ceased, we reorganized to continue our approach. Donahoo didn't get up. He was killed instantly. His young, clean face is as vivid to me now as it was then. He had not been with us more than two hours. He never had the need to take the rifle off his shoulder. We had not reached the front line, and the war was over for him before he'd had a chance to even to see the enemy. Yet, in the short period he was on Iwo, I felt his sacrifice was greater than those who spend years in the service yet are never exposed to enemy fire.

For many Marines, the war was over before they even saw the enemy. This picture of a dead Marine, taken by a Coast Guard combat photographer, represents the loss of one of America's "cream of the crop."

I knew Private Donahoo but for a brief time, yet he has remained in my memory throughout all these years—another example of the loss of one of America's "cream of the crop."

Chapter 8

The Hill That Opened

On about D plus eight, after capturing the knoll north of Airfield No. 2, we awaited further orders. I observed what might be our next objective, a hill to our front. While cautiously watching the enemy position, my mind pondered. Then, as in a dream, I thought I saw the side of the hill open like a door on its hinges and from its orifice come a large Japanese field piece being pushed on tracks by a crew of six or eight men. The field piece fired three rounds, which woke me out of my daze into the realization that perhaps this was not something I was imagining. As quickly as they fired the rounds, the Japanese pushed the big gun back into the hill. The opening closed and the Japanese and the field piece disappeared from sight. The whole thing had occurred so quickly I wasn't sure that I had seen it. Was it my imagination?

I was ashamed to tell my noncommissioned officer, Sgt. James Henry, what had happened for fear he might think that I had succumbed to battle fatigue, but I did ask him to concentrate on that same area without telling him what I had seen. I looked through my field glasses and patiently waited, and then it happened again. Sgt. Henry grabbed my arm and in a befuddled tone told me to look at the hill. There was no doubt about it. The two of us saw it. The big gun was pushed out, fired three more rounds to our right flank, and before we knew it, was pushed back into the side of the hill again. The doors were well camouflaged and blended in with the rest of the hill. We then realized why we were having such a difficult time locating the enemy's gun position. The enemy was so proficient at their task that the efficiency of the total operation was almost guaranteed. This, as well as the underground tunnels, proved that Japan's preparations for this island had been undertaken many years prior to the attack on Pearl Harbor.

Then I wondered, Why would the Japanese expose themselves when they knew that we were so close we would be able to see them? Why didn't they direct their fire on us instead of the ravine to our right? Both of these questions were soon answered: first, the gun emplacement was constructed to fire in just one direction along the ravine, which was the obvious approach to the hill. It was on tracks and in a fixed direction and could not rotate. Second, the Japanese were firing on I Company, which was coming to join us.

I knew that Lt. Raymond Ickes, who was commanding I Company, was unaware of the location of the gun, nor could he get to it even if he did know. Our ammunition was almost depleted, and it was too much of a gamble for us to exchange fire with the enemy. We had no fortification that could offer resistance to a big gun. I didn't want to further expose my men after what they had been through. At that moment I would have given anything for a bazooka. I called headquarters and informed Colonel Boehm about the situation. He put his 81-mm mortars at my disposal and put me in contact with the mortars crew. We waited for the side of the hill to open again. When it did, I gave the order for the mortars to fire, and phosphorous and explosive shells were dropped on the enemy emplacements. When our shelling stopped, the side of that hill had been opened for the last time. The crew had been killed and the gun was knocked out.

Lieutenant Ickes's unit eventually joined us on our right. He told me he had selected that ravine because it appeared to be the best protection for his men. By this time it was two o'clock in the afternoon and we still hadn't received the relief that had been promised. I tried to call headquarters, but my wires were cut again and the battery I had picked up earlier had gone dead. I told Lt. Baker to take charge and again went back to headquarters. Colonel Boehm replenished our supply of ammo and combined part of another unit with mine, then ordered us to stand by to move ahead again.

Raymond Ickes

Lt. Raymond Ickes, of Chicago, is an extraordinary person. His father was secretary of the interior under Pres. Franklin Roosevelt's New Deal Administration. Ickes had been in the FBI before joining the Marine Corps. The rest of us knew that he could have received special treatment with a high rank in any of the military services. He also could have comfortably waited out the war in Washington, D.C., but he chose to compete for a commission as a second lieutenant in the Marine Corps. He was commissioned and further chose to see action with a rifle company. Ickes and I were in the same battalion and on several occasions led platoons adjacent to each other.

While I waited for I Company to join us on our flank, Ickes received heavy fire from the enemy and was wounded.

Lt. Raymond Ickes, *left,* a nurse, and I hold a Japanese flag at the naval hospital in Aeia Heights, Honolulu, Hawaii, in April 1945. A master of seven languages, a judo expert, a brilliant attorney, and an interesting conversationalist, Lt. Ickes is the most unforgettable person I have ever met. Author's collection

I was close enough to go to him with Corpsman Young. He was shot through the lungs and could not move his left arm. The thing that really worried him wasn't his wound, but rather that he could not move his left arm, which would affect his ability to shoot in rifle tournaments in the future. He was a national rifle champion.

He was also a master of seven foreign languages, a judo expert, a brilliant attorney, and the most interesting conversationalist about any matter that one cared to discuss. After the war he was appointed special deputy attorney general and served at the Nuremberg Trials. He had met heads of state and knew the appointed governor of the territory of Hawaii on a first-name basis. I was in the hospital bed adjacent to his in Hawaii and saw several congressmen visit him, but to me, Ickes's most important visitor was Gen. Alexander Vandegrift, commandant of the Marine Corps. Ickes introduced me to him. I was thrilled to meet our top boss. One day Ickes asked me to accompany him to the hospital library. We browsed there for awhile, then I moved to one section and he to another. When we made our selections, I placed my books on the checkout counter. As I recall, one was about a sports legend and the other a historical novel. Ickes presented his three books to the librarian. I noticed that one was written in Japanese, one in Italian, and one in Spanish—quite a contrast from my selection. I jokingly asked him why he picked these titles. He remarked in earnest that he had met each of the authors and was interested in what they had to say. I should have realized that nothing he decided to do would phase me.

After the war we kept in touch for a few years. I returned to Western Maryland College for summer courses in 1946. Ickes and his wife at that time lived in the Washington, D.C., suburbs, not too far from the college. When they invited me to dinner one evening, Ickes led me on a tour of the premises. I was impressed by the trophy room. I saw trophies on a table and awards, medals, memorabilia, and Indian headdresses from various tribes designating him an honorary chief covering all four walls. He is the most unforgettable person I have ever met.

Chapter 9

Lunch with a Dead Man
and Other Thoughts

It was on Guam that I first saw someone killed in combat, a Japanese soldier just a few yards from me. Though he was the enemy and this was war, I was very upset. I tried hard to conceal my feelings from the others. Company Executive Officer Clyde McGinnis noticed I was disturbed by the sight of that first killing and suggested I would get used to it. But at that time it did not seem possible. It wasn't too long after that I first saw a fellow Marine killed by the enemy. My quick reaction as a witness to the death of a man I knew justified the killing of the enemy, which soon became commonplace.

By contrast, in a crater on Iwo, I opened a box of rations and started to eat. With me was a dead Japanese soldier. By this time, my appetite was not deterred by the company of a dead man.

I soon became a seasoned combat Marine and developed the reasoning that one must kill or be killed. Whenever we killed one of the enemy our feeling was, "There is one who won't raise a son to kill mine."

It is difficult to describe the sensation of seeing the enemy eye to eye as he raises his rifle at you. You freeze for a brief moment, then the adrenaline flows and you quickly try to get him before he gets you. This soon becomes instinctive. I worried that this feeling of demeaning life would pervade after the war, that is, if I lasted long enough to become a civilian again. The truth is, after the war I did not go hunting again. The very thought of it is still distasteful to me.

One moonlit night while on watch in my foxhole, I observed a rocky ledge off to my left. Somehow, I did not notice it in the daylight when we dug in. It concerned me because the enemy could use it as an approach to our position.

As I stared at it in the moonlight, the outline of the rock resembled the face of a man—a profile silhouette with distinct features of forehead, nose, and chin. I thought of Mt. Rushmore's George Washington, except this was a side view, not frontal. I was sure the figure was looking at me, but I didn't know if it was friend or foe, whether it was there to protect us or to attack us. This became more convincing as I continued to look at it. Iwo could do something like that to you.

It was a long night and the sky was clear and peaceful except for the Japanese artillery and sporadic bursts of gunfire. As dawn approached, the silhouette gradually faded and the characteristic form of the rocky ledge began to assume its natural daytime appearance. The profile was no longer distinguishable. I facetiously thought the figure must be nocturnal. We resumed our attack and moved on and away from the ledge, but not from the impression and concern that stuck with me.

Our days were preoccupied with the enemy, with no time or reason for personal concerns. The nights were dreadfully long and provided more than ample opportunity for the mind to ramble.

Two men shared a foxhole; one watched and listened while the other tried to sleep or rest. We alternated every hour or so. In order to remain awake while on watch, I had to keep my mind active and alert, my eyes open to look, and my ears tuned to listen. That's when the mind went to work, and it never seemed to slow down.

During these periods of vigil, my thoughts carried me randomly from one topic to another. At times related, sometimes not, they invariably came to rest on thoughts about my family: what they were doing back home; my kid brother in the Army Air Force, shot down over Germany and listed as missing in action; my other brother in the China-Burma-India theater of operations; my brother-in-law in Europe under General Patton; my sister handling the correspondence for all of us and holding the fort for my parents.

Sitting and waiting for day to break did lend itself to serious soul searching. I questioned myself, Was this really happening or was it a nightmare in hell? A few close artillery shells or the *rat-tat-tat* of machine gun fire soon settled that issue.

My mind traversed the spectrum of my past: school and college, and how final exams were so critical—until Iwo; why making the football team was so essential—until Iwo; how making a good impression on a date was so important—until Iwo; how getting a job during summer vacations was so significant—until Iwo; what's in store for my future. My future? Iwo is my present and future. . . .

To remain awake during my vigil, I would force myself to focus on a trivial thought or perform an exercise, such as enumerating the various functions of my helmet. Was there anything of greater utilitarian value than my steel helmet? I could use it as a bucket to wash my clothes or catch rainfall for fresh water, for shaving, or as a wash basin; as a shovel to dig a foxhole; as a seat, or a pot over a fire, and, of course, as protection from enemy fire. Insignificant thoughts became significant.

Then my thoughts would stray back to home and the reports they might be receiving about this battle. Did my parents receive the erroneous notice that I was missing in action as reported by 1st Sergeant Moore after that first night when my platoon was isolated from the rest of K Company? How many more casualties would we suffer before the end? What

U.S. Marines kneel in prayer at Catholic services during a lull in the fighting for control of the island near Airfield No. 1. On Iwo Jima, for the first time in my life, I understood and felt the impact of prayer.

about my buddies who were hit and those who might be next? Would I leave this island alive and intact? Are my folks okay?

Families back home suffered on a daily basis from stress, anxiety, fear, and strain. Their only solace was hope, faith, and prayer. I reflected on the value of religion and prayer and my relationship to God. On Iwo, for the first time in my life, I understood and felt the impact of prayer. My mind dwelt on the importance of each word. I visualized the complete meaning and concept of the prayers I had been taught by rote as a child but whose substance I'd been unable to reflect on until now.

Part 4

Heading North

Chapter 10

Motoyama Village and Beyond

As we pushed northward to capture the island, we came across the village of Motoyama, which contained a sulfur mine. The smoldering smoke eking out of the cracks and creeping along the ground was an eerie sight. The fumes seemed to cling within a few feet of the ground and gave off a pungent, disagreeable odor. It made me feel as if I were in a Hollywood setting for a horror picture, except we also had to contend with real live Japanese soldiers who were shooting real bullets.

While going through the village we came across the remains of what may have been a structure used for meetings or instruction, perhaps a classroom for families and children of the construction workers fortifying the island. We found maps, booklets, and leaflets written in Japanese, showing the enemy's success in taking the islands in the Pacific. A map of the United States indicated that they were in control of some of our coastline. It depicted their planes sinking our war ships. There also were illustrations showing children at play or work.

On another day while on patrol I rested against a ledge about a foot above the ground. I leaned over to pick up a bullet and noticed a slight opening at the bottom of the ledge. Fortunately, it turned out to be a vacated pillbox, so well concealed and camouflaged that I did not recognize it even as I sat on it.

One early morning as we were getting ready to move on to the next hill, I saw several Marines a few hundred yards to our left. They were folding their blankets at about the time we were ready to move out. We waved to each other. As we started forward, they began traveling in the same general direction as we did. I assumed they were members of a unit that had come during the night to join us, although I was not aware of any outfit in that location. As we walked on, they came closer and closer to us. When they were about thirty yards away, they opened fire. They were immediately subdued by our platoon, and when we got to them, we saw that they were Japanese dressed in Marine clothing. In an effort to confuse us, the enemy often wore the uniforms of the Marines they had killed.

There were many occasions when the Japanese would try to provoke us to disclose our position in the dark by yelling in perfect English, "Corpsman, help me; I'm hit!" Any red-blooded Marine or corpsman would run to the cries of a fellow Marine who was injured. In these instances, however, those who cried for help were the Japanese who waited with cocked rifles for our corpsman to show his face. I also remember hearing them shout derogatory adjectives about Babe Ruth, Joe Louis, or President Roosevelt, demeaning their images. They hoped we would charge out of our positions to protest their insults.

Chapter 11

Night Attack on Hill 362-C

For military purposes, hills are identified by their elevation in feet. There were three Hills 362 on Iwo, all very troublesome. Hill 362-C was several hundred yards to our front, but the enemy emplacements controlled the open ground between us so well that for three days we were knocked back every time we tried to take it. Even our supporting fire from heavy artillery, naval vessels, and planes could not dent their defenses.

Following the third unsuccessful day of our attack on Hill 362-C, Colonel Boehm summoned the battalion officers to his command post at about midnight. A meeting at this time was highly unusual, and there was a great deal of speculation concerning its significance. Colonel Boehm notified us that our division commander, Gen. Graves B. Erskine, decided to take Hill 362-C that night. The plan was to take the hill and at daybreak continue the pursuit to the coast. This was to be the Marines' first attempt at aggressive night fighting in the war. The general planned the unexpected move as a surprise attack. Since we had never attacked at night, he was hoping that the enemy would be caught off guard.

Along with L Company of our battalion and units of the Twenty-first Regiment, we were assigned to lead the assault. My unit was on the right flank with L Company to our left. We assembled our units at about 0300 (3:00 A.M.) and prepared for this unique attack. It was a moonless night; therefore, we could not see the hill. This was fine because it also meant that the Japanese would not be able to see us as we moved toward them. We suspended the use of flares and illuminating shells so that we might attain the element of surprise. To keep our movement quiet, it was decided not to request supporting or preparatory fire, and we refrained from the use of radio or walkie-talkie. Silence was mandatory.

We formed a human chain abreast of each other and advanced in complete darkness, relying only on our luminous compass. Just as we took off I heard several machine gun bursts to our left. L Company responded and that ended the exchange. I suspected that this short exchange of fire would reveal our movement to the enemy, but apparently it did not. I could vaguely see the silhouette of Hill 362-C as we proceeded.

With confidence we advanced toward the hill. It all seemed too easy. We reached the objective without an incident, except for that short exchange. As day broke, I began to identify our newly acquired position in relation to the rest of the immediate terrain and woefully realized that we had missed our objective. By misjudging the distance and direction, we had taken Hill 331 instead of 362-C, which was over one hundred yards away.

The Japanese soldiers on Hill 331 were unsuspecting of our presence as they casually moved about their positions. We startled them and began to pick them off rather easily before they realized what was happening. Then the fighting began at very close range. At times, we were firing at a distance of only twenty yards or so—just about the width of an average street—close enough to clearly see their faces. I recall exchanging fire with one of the enemy. He fired at me and missed. I fired at him and he ducked behind a rock. He popped up and fired again. I returned the fire. He raised himself once more to shoot again. I couldn't understand how I could have missed him. Was he the same person, or another who just looked like him? I wasn't sure since, in the heat of battle, all the enemy looked alike.

Within a couple of hours we had subdued their fire and continued on to Hill 362-C. There we received fire from the front and sides, and from the enemy positions we had bypassed during the night. There were as many Japanese behind us as in front of us. We were surrounded and in a desperate situation. Again we were physically cut off from the rest of the battalion. Along with L Company, we were the assault unit and were caught in a trap. By about 1400 (2:00 P.M.), our artillery proved too much for them and we succeeded in taking the hill.

Only under the cover of darkness were we able to move across the open terrain. Hill 362-C, whose capture had stalled our momentum for three days, was taken in this unconventional manner. Our casualties during these three days were staggering, but once we controlled the hill, we felt the rest would be relatively easy because we now occupied all the high land on the island. All considered, this, our first night attack in the Pacific war, was a successful venture.

Bill Terrill

Cpl. Bill Terrill, of Port Angeles, Washington, was nineteen years old when we landed on Iwo. As a K Company 60-mm

Cpl. Bill Terrill, K Company mortar man. On Veterans Day 1995, fifty years after the battle, he received the Purple Heart medal as a result of his wounds at Iwo Jima. Twenty-seven Medals of Honor were awarded to Marine and Navy servicemen of Iwo Jima—more than for any other single battle in naval history. Courtesy of Bill Terrill

mortar gunner, he remembers looking up at Mt. Suribachi and seeing our flag waving in the breeze. "The sight was encouraging, but I knew the real fight was just beginning. We had a long way to go," he remembers.

We were ordered to take our position between the Fourth and Fifth Divisions and advance through the middle up to the north end. "We were firing mortars in support of our rifle platoons," Terrill said. "We moved onto the airstrip. We got about almost half across the runway and all hell broke loose. Men were getting hit all around me. Captain Crawford, our company commander, was killed. It was bad for our morale since he was well liked as a man and leader. I am told that we lost four of our six officers and over one hundred men across the strip. A Jap 47 antitank gun fired and I picked up two pieces of shrapnel in my right leg. The corpsman sent me to the aid station and I was there about three or four hours getting the metal taken out. I consider myself a lucky guy. When I returned to my outfit, we were on the southeast side of the airfield, dug in, and Lieutenant Caruso was in command of the company. We regrouped that night and for the next three days we proceeded to take the airstrip. We then moved north with what we had left.

"One night we were dug in and Russell Boydston was in a foxhole close to mine. We were all rotating sleep (one awake all the time). In the middle of the night, I heard a lot of screaming coming from Russell's foxhole. A Jap had jumped in the foxhole with him and Russell had beat him with his entrenching tool until the Jap was dead. The incident badly effected [sic] him. He had to be taken back to the ship. This was a very sorry situation. I shall never be able to erase this memory.

"Later in the campaign when we advanced to the upper half of Iwo, we had trouble taking Hill 362-C. We made a third try, only this time it was a night attack. We did not know what was going on when we moved out in the middle of the night, but when daylight came, we found that we were into their lines approximately two hundred and fifty yards as I understood it. There was no talking or firing so the orders went. It was a very tense situation! We had broken their lines and knew we had been successful. Later we reported taking the wrong hill . . . but we had broken their lines and that was what mattered the most to us. But then a real firefight erupted as we thought we had reached Hill 362-C, but we hadn't, at least not until later that day.

"A memory that shall forever stay with me is the day that Sergeant James Henry was killed. He had been forward observing and relaying orders to the mortars. We only had enough men left to fire two of the mortars. I heard Lieutenant Caruso yell back to us, 'Henry down!' He had been shot in the head. It was bad, there was not any way that he could survive. I will never forget the look in his eyes.

"Somewhere before we got to the third airstrip, we dug in on a flat area. Japs were all over the place and we were ordered to fire mortar flares every five minutes to light up the front. They were trying to break our lines to get badly needed water. A young replacement was in the hole with me. His name was Yuksic. We took turns sleeping and firing the flares. Sometime during the night, I noticed a Jap coming toward our hole. I am sure he had seen our muzzle blast. I took my carbine and woke Yuksic so he could fire flares. When the Jap was about three feet from us, I emptied my rifle. We were both a couple of scared Marines, to say the least.

"Lieutenant Caruso gave the order to Bill Alcola (from Colorado) and me to go over toward Cushman Pocket (which was about two hundred and fifty yards from us) and see if there were any Fourth Division Marines there possibly wounded. We took two-way radios so when we reached our destination, we were able to radio back that we had found two badly wounded men and another luckily not hit. Lieutenant Caruso told us to stay there and that he would send a tank up and for us to get the two wounded Marines up through the escape hatch, since they could not be carried out as it was too dangerous. Within an hour, we were able to hear the tank arriving. They drove over our hole and we put the two injured Marines up into the hatch. The three of us made it back to K Company feeling good for what we had done.

"We had lost so many men, we kept receiving replacements, which was of some help. After the island was secured, we returned to Guam. Only eleven of the original two hundred thirty men remained."

In the summer of 1995, after fifty years, I received a letter from Bill Terrill. He explained he had learned from a friend that he should have received the Purple Heart.

Terrill had assumed that since he was not hospitalized for his injury, he did not qualify for the medal. He wrote to Marine headquarters to ascertain an official decision. They notified him that if the shrapnel pierced the skin, even if it did not require hospitalization, he was eligible to receive the Purple Heart medal. Because there was no written record of his injury, however, it would require an affidavit from his commanding officer or someone in authority at that time.

I was his mortar officer at that time. He, however, had no indication of my whereabouts, except that I lived in New Jersey. Through a friend, he came across the article I wrote for the Associated Press commemorating the twenty-fifth anniversary of the battle of Iwo Jima. The article mentioned that I was a public school administrator in New Jersey. Terrill eventually tracked me down via the teachers' pension office, assuming that I must have retired after all these years.

I did remember the incident and immediately verified it. Terrill received the Purple Heart medal at a special ceremony on Veterans Day 1995, at an area navy base—fifty years after the fact.

Fourth Division Marines dash from landing craft on the beach at Iwo Jima, February 19, 1945. AP Newsfeatures photo.

Marine Corps amtracs and medium tanks hit by Japanese fire and bogged down in loose beach sand are scavenged for parts and supplies, February 26, 1945. Official U.S. Marine Corps photo.

Pvt. Robert Olney of Waltham, Massachusetts, digs for his rifle after being buried by a Japanese artillery round.

Marines regroup after taking a Japanese pillbox (center background). AP Newsfeatures photo.

U.S. troops take shelter as friendly fire pummels enemy strongholds. AP Newsfeatures photo.

This enemy soldier, thought to be dead for more than a day and a half, was taken prisoner when advancing Marines found he was still breathing. A live grenade can be seen a few inches from his right hand. This man was the first enemy prisoner taken on Iwo Jima. *Leatherneck* magazine photo from Acme.

A wounded Marine is evacuated toward offshore U.S. Naval fleet. AP Newsfeatures photo by Joe Rosenthal.

Wounded Marines are loaded onto aircraft at Motoyama airstrip for evacuation to base hospitals. Official U.S. Marine Corps photo by T/Sgt. H. N. Gillespie.

Chapter 12

Know Thine Enemy

We had a gross misconception of the enemy before we encountered them. Since the bombing of Pearl Harbor and throughout the war, our media created a distorted image of the Japanese fighters and their leaders.

Newspapers and magazine cartoons caricatured the enemy as inhuman, inferior, puny, wearing oversized, horned-rim glasses, resembling bespectacled monkeys. Japan's leaders were pictured as bungling idiots, incompetent, unimaginative, and inefficient planners. Comedians targeted the enemy as objects of their jokes, and songwriters attributed words of ridicule and belittlement to them, creating the impression that they were pushovers.

These image molders led us to believe we were fighting a third-rate, ill-trained enemy with outdated equipment and ineffective weaponry. None of this was true. To the contrary, the Japanese fighters were well-trained, combat-wise, expert marksmen, well disciplined, ingenious, uncanny, crafty, and programmed to fight and die for their ultimate purpose: their duty to their emperor.

We certainly underestimated their ability and misunderstood their extreme loyalty and dedication to the emperor. They were not at all what our image molders back home made them out to be. They were not jokes; they were not inept. We hated them enough to kill them, but we did respect their ability. I often thought if we had to go to war again, I would want them on our side.

They were not puny. I was surprised to see so many of them six feet tall and weighing more than two hundred pounds. Later, I was informed that these were the Imperial forces, whose special assignment was the defense of their homeland. Since Iwo Jima was the doorway to Japan's mainland, this explained their presence on the island.

I did not see many Japanese wearing glasses. They were persistent and patient; they could hide and wait hours and even days before they would fire a single shot to hit their designated target. I recall the interrogation of a Japanese prisoner in which he explained how they could identify— and thus eliminate—the commanding officer by observing which foxhole was visited most frequently or if he was followed by a radio man or a messenger. It was not just a coincidence that many of our officers were shot through the head with high-powered rifles. We also learned that the Japanese were trained to shoot us in the legs, making us immobile. This would force other Marines to expose themselves as they came out to our rescue. Our men who were retrieving the wounded became easy prey.

Our training emphasized the concept of chain of command. When a leader became a casualty, the next in line of command immediately assumed the responsibility of leadership. This enabled the mission to continue without interruption. The Japanese philosophy ignored that premise because they refused to accept the fact that they were dispensable. Consequently, when their leaders were killed or wounded, the others fought as disorganized small bands or as individuals—though ferocious and tenacious.

The Japanese were aware of our pattern of life and capitalized on it. They constantly disrupted our nights by intermittent artillery barrages, rifle fire, and counterattacks in an effort to make us ineffective the following day. After a few days their harassment took its toll on us.

What made the Japanese warrior so ready and willing to sacrifice his life for his emperor? What made him so dedicated and obedient at any cost?

It was startling to learn how and why the Japanese became submissive in their self-sacrificing devotion, completely dedicated in body and soul. It did not begin with Emperor Hirohito; he was one in a continuous line of succession, dating back some twenty-five hundred years, of descendants from the Sun Goddess. The rising sun on Japan's flags, ships, planes, tanks, and the like symbolized and furthered the premise of the emperor's direct relationship to the Sun Goddess. Many Japanese fighting men wrapped the rising sun flag around their body as they went into battle. This was to strengthen their resolve as well as express their devotion to the emperor.

Hirohito was revered as a living god. Considered to be of divine nature, he was not subject in any way to his people. He was above all of them and beyond reproach in wisdom and in all matters pertaining to education, the government, the military, and religion. He was his people's source of inspiration and commanded their full devotion and commitment in life and death. By comparison, President

Roosevelt was not our idol. We did not owe our life to him. We did not fight for him or his honor, or any political symbol, or any material object. We did, indeed, fight for our own survival, for our families, our buddies, and our way of life. These served to inspire and motivate us to victory.

The emperor's deity demanded that no one was worthy to touch him. Doctors, dentists, and others had to wear gloves in treating him. His tailor could only estimate his measurements. His clothes were worn only once. His subjects had to "look up" to him. He was seldom viewed in public unless on a high platform or on his horse. His white horse symbolized divine purity; his military attire stressed the combination of his divinity and earthly position. Not even his wife was permitted to walk ahead or abreast of him.

The emperor could not be questioned in any way, shape, or form; this was the blueprint for his subjects' unchallenged loyalty, dedication, obedience, service, duty, and sacrifice. To that end, from an early age Japanese children received religious indoctrination and military training, which were nurtured throughout their lives. Complete compliance with the emperor's cause was not only of the highest importance, it was the only purpose. To be prepared to die for him demonstrated obedience and personal honor deserving of ultimate heavenly reward.

Japanese military training omitted any reference to surrender or defeat. Because they were fighting for their living god-on-earth, victory was assured. Should any one of them surrender, not only would he be dishonored, but his family would be ostracized. His alternative was suicidal kamikaze or banzai attacks, or hara-kiri (ritual suicide). This was evidenced by the fact that rather than give up even against insurmountable odds, many chose to join banzai attacks:

small bands of the enemy would charge into a company of Marines, acknowledging certain death. Many hid in the jungles or bush or caves even after the war was over. One Japanese soldier on Guam hid for twenty years rather than surrender or be captured.

When it became evident that Japan would lose Iwo Jima, Tokyo notified the commanding officer, Lieutenant General Kuribayashi, that no help would be forthcoming. The general told his troops that they were to die an honorable death for the emperor and that each was expected to take ten Marines along with him.

When Hiroshima was bombed on August 6, 1945, Hirohito refused to surrender, necessitating the dropping of a second bomb three days later on Nagasaki. Even then the emperor hesitated. The odious meaning of the word surrender prevailed right to the top. In his statements acknowledging Japan's defeat, Hirohito refused to mention the word surrender, stating instead that he had brought the war to an end to "prevent further inhumanities."

The Japanese believed that they were invincible and would not be captured, but that in the event they were, their capture would represent the ultimate disgrace for them as well as their families. They were told that as prisoners of war they would be severely tortured and that capture or surrender at the hands of Marines would be worse, because to be accepted in the Marine Corps, one had had to prove one's ruthlessness by killing a member of one's family.

As a result of this indoctrination, rather than surrender even in the face of impossible odds, the Japanese savagely fought to the death. At times, they came out of their lines with arms raised high, waving a white flag as a signal of surrender. As they approached us, however, they would detonate the charge of explosives tied to their bodies in an attempt

Marines carefully remove a Japanese prisoner. Many Japanese booby-trapped themselves with explosives or otherwise sacrificed their lives in suicide missions rather than surrender. Consequently, few were taken prisoner—the ultimate disgrace. Out of approximately twenty-one thousand Japanese Imperial Guards on the island, about one thousand were prisoners of war.

to kill us as well as themselves. By booby-trapping themselves, they believed they would be spared the anticipated torture and would fulfill their mission in life, thus gaining entitlement to their hereafter.

Consequently, taking a Japanese prisoner was difficult and rare. I remember one who was caught off guard and captured. He went down on his knees and lowered his head to the ground. He asked the interrogator not to torture him but to kill him instantly. The interpreter explained that he was not going to be tortured or killed, and instead gave the prisoner a cigarette and placed him at ease. Whereas we were instructed that if we were taken prisoner, we were required only to reveal our name, rank, and serial number, the Japanese were not advised or prepared in the event of capture. Thus this prisoner willingly provided any military information requested by the interrogator. He bragged about their strength, their units, their leaders, their movement and plans. Therefore, information derived from a prisoner was of paramount importance. Battle-seasoned Marines found it difficult, however, to restrain themselves from firing at the enemy even if he showed signs of surrender. We would not know if he was booby-trapped until it was too late. We took no chances.

Part 5

The Last Patrol

Chapter 13

Wounded

After capturing Hill 362-C, we managed to push to the northern end of the island and reach the ocean, our battalion having the distinction of being the first to reach the north beach. K Company probably had only 50 of the original 230 men left by this time. I Company and L Company of our battalion were hit just about as badly as we were, so the three companies, assisted by the remnants of B Company of the Twenty-first Regiment of the Third Marine Division, secured a position on the high cliffs overlooking the sea to the northeast. We now felt that all we had to do was to wait for the adjacent units to catch up to us and the campaign would be over. The sight of the ocean from that cliff is what all of us had struggled for, and for which many of us had been killed. Originally, it was a question of how long it would take before reaching the other end of the island. Then it became a question of how many would be alive by the time it was reached. Now it was ours. It had required nothing less than the fiercest fighting of the war to reach this objective.

Those of us who were left were exuberant but displayed mixed emotions; we were glad for ourselves but sad for those who did not make it. We now had a new lease on life. No longer did we look like the walking dead. No longer did we remain motionless and expressionless for spells of time (the Asiatic stare is what we called it); anticipating proper food and rest, we talked about getting aboard ship, enjoying a prolonged shower, eating a hot meal, and sleeping. Everyone's interest in life was restored.

Some of the men filled their canteens with salt water to prove that we had reached the end of the island. We spoke about our return to Guam and discussed some changes for our camp. We even received word from the higher echelon of a "job well done," and were notified to hold our position on the cliff until the flanking units were abreast of us. We were not to move out again—just sit and wait until the others could join us—then it would all be over. It seemed too good to be true; at last, we had achieved the final phase.

But our peace and jubilation lasted only a few hours. There was no sign of an adjacent unit. Colonel Boehm ordered me to take out a two-platoon patrol to assist the unit on our right to move up. Our mission was to wipe out the caves that were holding back the advance of the flank company.

The Japanese had retreated to a network of connected caves in the northern cliffs, where they were lying in wait for the advancing Marines. The colonel advised me that another battalion had sustained heavy losses in that area the previous day. He added that the Marine detail that had gone out to retrieve their dead and wounded had reported that the bodies were gone and that there were signs that they had been dragged into the caves. He stated the obvious conclusion: the Japanese were desperate for food and water because their supply line had been cut off from the outset of the battle and thus had resorted to acts of cannibalism. I received my instructions and relayed them to Sgt. Gordon Schisel and told him to get the men ready to move out at any moment. Sergeant Schisel acknowledged and said, "You know, Lieutenant, all the men who

The northern caves. Lt. Gen. Tadamichi Kuribayashi supervised the construction of an intricate maze of caves on Iwo Jima. As our forces advanced, the Japanese retreated to the caves in the northern cliffs where the lieutenant general's headquarters was located. The 150-foot-long headquarters was protected beneath 75 feet of solid rock and reached only by way of a 500-foot tunnel.

are here now have come all the way. Wouldn't it be hell if someone were to get hurt on a little patrol like this, especially after reaching this north beach?" I agreed with him, but at the same time didn't think much of the risk. My preference was to get it over in a hurry.

Lt. "Red" Baker's platoon and mine were united for the patrol, probably twenty-five to thirty men in all. I was placed in charge and had the radio for communications with battalion headquarters. I was to lead the patrol and Sergeant Schisel would bring up the rear. We reviewed our attack plans and took off into the open end of a horseshoe-shaped area. About one hundred yards of the approach was covered, with no sign of the enemy. All the caves thus far had been checked by flame throwers with negative results.

The flame thrower was the weapon the Japanese feared most—at least that was the only one that made them yell and run. They were unafraid of our mortar shells; they charged into a curtain of our bullets; they tossed grenades back to us; they shoved pole charges back through the openings of pillboxes. But the fearsome flame thrower caused them to panic.

It must be noted that the flame thrower not only burns, but its heat is so intense it consumes the oxygen within an enclosure, such as a pillbox or bunker. The occupants die by suffocation, not fire.

By shooting the flame into an opening of a cave, all other openings connected to it would emit smoke or fire. By this method we were able to ascertain the chain of connecting caves. They had been built as clusters to protect their segments by flanking crossfire. Our flame throwers eliminated this purpose. It was the unsung weaponry of the campaign, coming into its own by virtue of Iwo Jima's characteristic fortification of tunnels, caves, pillboxes, and bunkers—all areas of confinement of space and oxygen.

Before moving ahead to the area of my assignment—to clean out the enemy-infested caves—I consulted with Lt. Herb Smith, whose zone was nearby, for whatever information he could pass on to me. Lieutenant Smith, of Tennessee, was an officer of L Company. At one point in time, he was the only original officer left in that company. Along with Lt. Ray Overpeck, of Kansas, the only surviving officer of I Company, and I, the only surviving officer of K Company, the three of us represented what remained of the battalion's original twenty-two line officers. We shared a sense of guilt or shame in not having been wounded or killed.

After receiving the information I needed from Lieutenant Smith, we talked about our heavy losses and the fact that only one of the original officers of each of the three companies in the battalion was left. Three days later Smith left the battalion command post and headed for his company. It was the last time he was seen. He was reported missing in action. One day after his disappearance, Lieutenant Overpeck, the lone survivor of the battalion, was shot through the hip. The Third Battalion of the Ninth Marine Regiment lost all twenty-two company officers who had originally landed on Iwo Jima. Nine were killed, one was missing in action, and twelve were wounded.

The roll call of company officers of the Third Battalion, Ninth Marine Regiment, would appear as follows:

I COMPANY

Evers, Capt. William C.	killed
Ickes, Lt. Raymond W.	wounded
Jones, Lt. Harry W.	killed
Kristoferson, Lt. Alfred E.	wounded
Overpeck, Lt. Raymond A.	wounded
Scanlon, Lt. William P.	killed
Smith, Lt. Alexander B.	wounded

K COMPANY

Crawford, Capt. William K.	killed
Baker, Lt. John C.	killed
Caruso, Lt. Patrick F.	wounded
McGinnis, Lt. Clyde R.	wounded
Rasmussen, Lt. Andrew P.	wounded
Roney, Lt. Robert H.	wounded
Thompson, Lt. David E.	wounded
Thompson, Lt. Kenneth R.	killed

L COMPANY

Lewis, Capt. David H.	wounded
Brower, Lt. John W.	killed
Cunha, WO Ulysses F.	wounded
Pollak, Lt. Dale S.	killed
Scott, Lt. Hayden A.	wounded
Smith, Lt. Herbert G.	missing
Wright, Lt. David W.	killed

I don't know how many of the enlisted men of I Company or L Company survived by this time. I know they suffered heavily. Of the original 230 enlisted men of K Company, only 15 or so had made it this far.

K Company. *Above, top row, left,* Lt. Clyde McGinnis. *Bottom row, left to right,* Lts. Robert H. Roney, Dave Thompson, and I in Guam in 1944 and *below, same order,* at the 1975 reunion in New Orleans. In 1970, the Associated Press published my account of the battle to commemorate the twenty-fifth anniversary of the campaign. Since then many survivors and their families have attended the annual reunions. Author's collection

There was no doubt we would take the island. The question was how much longer and how many more casualties it would require.

We now moved into the next sector. I started to believe that we would be back to our cliff sooner than we thought, that the Japanese who had occupied these caves merely had retreated when they saw us coming and probably had withdrawn to a more secure position.

We continued to move ahead, not knowing what to expect, with still no visible sign of the enemy. I thought it a bit strange that the Japanese hadn't greeted us to this point, but I didn't mind their oversight. If we reached our objective and encountered no enemy, that would be fine with me. We could return, report no casualties, and rejoin the battalion.

When we were just about halfway to our objective, my forward scout told me that he noticed a flash near the entrance of a cave directly to our front. I signaled the patrol to stop and take cover. We assumed that the flash was the reflection of a rifle barrel in the sun, but with hundreds of cave openings all around us it was almost impossible to identify that particular one by pointing to it. To pinpoint the precise cave, I asked the scout to fire a few tracer bullets into it. Just as he did, a Japanese soldier fired and hit him through the helmet. The bullet penetrated the helmet but miraculously only grazed the side of his head. Blood oozed out but the scout remained conscious. Before he could explain to me where he had seen the enemy, they opened fire on us. In a split second, a medley of Japanese artillery, rockets, mortars, and small arms was synchronized into devastating firepower from the front and both sides. Most of the patrol was under this heavy fire, while others proceeded with the plan as arranged. The first squad was led by Cpl. Jerry Kizer, from Brownsville, Tennessee. He knew that I wanted him to continue to the right of the enemy position and to take them from the flank as the rest provided support from the front. He noticed me looking for him as I gave him the "go-ahead" sign.

Although we had endured some thirteen continuous, furious, restless, endless days of the most violent fighting, we were in the highest of spirits. We were eager to get this skirmish over with as quickly as we could to enable the adjacent unit to join us.

Corporal Kizer advanced his squad halfway to his designated position. More enemy rifle and machine guns rang out. The enemy had not evacuated the caves as I had thought. The intensity of their firepower increased so much that I realized there were many more than Colonel Boehm or the rest of us had anticipated. It was apparent that we were greatly outnumbered. The Japanese were clever enough to know we had to go into the caves after them. Therefore, they waited until we were close enough to draw us into an ambush and envelop as many of us as possible. We were sucked into the trap. If our scout had not seen them when he did, we would have gone in closer, making their catch even more lucrative. They had us where they wanted us; and both of us knew it.

The enemy fire was so abundant I could hardly pick my head up to see what was going on. Although the men realized the difficult situation we were in, we still intended to accomplish our objective as planned. Colonel Boehm, looking down from his command post, observed our predicament. He called me on the radio and ordered me to return to the company area because there were too many Japanese for our patrol to handle. I can still hear him yelling, "King 2, bring the patrol back—if it takes you all day and night, don't go any farther. King 2, bring the men back." His message altered our plans too suddenly and too radically. I had to contact the entire patrol and especially Corporal Kizer's squad, which had already gone around to flank the enemy. The patrol was spread over the area, and I had no means of communication with Lieutenant Baker on my left, or with Sergeant Schisel, who controlled the rear of my platoon, or with Corporal Kizer. All had to be alerted to our change of plan.

I regretted hearing the colonel's order to withdraw the patrol. I felt that aerial and naval support could have helped our cause to continue the pursuit. To withdraw now would mean to postpone the end. We could also expect plenty of fanatical banzai attacks or enemy infiltration that night if we did not continue the attack and knock out the enemy right then and there. But Colonel Boehm had ordered me to come back, and regardless of my own opinions, I had to execute his command as efficiently and as promptly as I was able, with minimum casualties.

We learned later that the colonel's order had probably saved the lives of our entire patrol. Although none of us knew it then, there were over three hundred Japanese in connecting caves waiting for our patrol to continue our advance into their pocket of death. The colonel's decision was God sent.

I had to establish contact with the other elements to start our withdrawal. Relayed from man to man, the word reached my former college classmate, Lt. Red Baker. I received his acknowledgment of the change via the same method. Baker ordered his platoon to give supporting fire to keep the enemy shooting at a minimum while I endeavored to contact Corporal Kizer's squad. Finally, I reached the last man of his column, Pfc. Joe D'Amico. I explained the new orders to him and had him pass it up to Kizer so we could start an orderly withdrawal. The theory, in simple terms, was for one part of the patrol to withdraw as the others fired at the enemy positions. The sections of the patrol would alternate the movements until we had completely pulled out. This would not be easy because the terrain there was flat and offered no protection from the view and fire of the enemy.

It must have been about 1530 (3:30 P.M.) on that afternoon of March 10 as we started to pull back. The Japanese apparently did not approve of our revised plan to withdraw and were about to protest our possible escape. When they saw we were not advancing toward their caves, they rendered even more firepower. They hoped to nail us before we completely withdrew. Colonel Boehm observed this and ordered 37-mm antitank guns and 81-mm mortars to neutralize their fire in order to facilitate our withdrawal. Our 81s lobbed many smoke shells to screen us from the enemy's view, but their weapons continued to fire at a rapid rate. They knew where we were.

How well I remember that particular scene. We were in their pocket, receiving their crossfire, pinned down and motionless with nothing to do but hug that dirt and wait for an opportunity to move again. I felt the intensity of the sun beating on me. It was shining brilliantly, baking the volcanic grit on my hands and face. A cool breeze came in from the ocean just a few hundred yards away. I welcomed it. It felt good, but the sun refused to yield to the breeze and increased its intensity. The dirt on my face was being cooked by the sun, and I wondered if I would live long enough to wash it clean again.

A long hour must have passed before the enemy firing had diminished. We managed to withdraw a bit. In the meantime, Corporal Kizer's squad had returned to us. There was still a good deal of open ground for us to travel back to the company area. Although the enemy firing had relented, I knew this little struggle wasn't over yet. I could see that Lieutenant Baker's half of the patrol had returned part of the way but were losing physical contact with my flank men. Because they were not subject to the enemy's firepower as my men were, they withdrew in long and rapid bounds. Also, Baker could not see our movements as well as we could see his, and I was concerned that he might leave us stranded without realizing it. Since his patrol did not have a phone or radio, my only means of communication with Baker was by messenger. I, however, had already sent my messenger back to the company area with instructions to inform the command post of the situation in detail. Rather than send Corporal Kizer, who had just returned from his sector, I yelled to him that I would run to Baker's unit and that he should withdraw the rest as best as he could until I got back.

The distance to Lieutenant Baker's position was probably half the length of a football field. I started running, zigzagging, and jumping into shell craters to stay out of the enemy's gun sights. Because of my temporary exuberant spirit, I felt charged in running that open terrain. Shots continued to ring out around me and because the enemy did not hit me, almost as a challenge, I lengthened the intervals between my stops. I don't really know what possessed me to do that, but I'll attribute it to the anticipation of the long, hard-fought victory that was about to be ours. Perhaps some of Lt. Alex Smith's bravado rubbed off on me at that time.

Alex "Smitty" Smith, former Ivy League football star, was in charge of the Third Battalion 81-mm mortars. Smith was amiable, cheerful, and always ready to offer a helping hand. He was a seasoned combatant. There seemed to be an aura about him and an indistinguishable thin line separating carelessness and fearlessness.

One morning when we had taken an objective on a ridge, Smith appeared to brazenly challenge the Japanese by subjecting himself to their fire. While the rest of us took cover, he stood out there proudly on the horizon, lighting a cigar as he casually surveyed the terrain. He began to pace the area, puffing on his cigar. I remember calling to him, "Get down, Smitty, you'll get hit. You're not strolling in the park." He yelled back, "No, the bastards can't hit me." I think he was sending them a message: "I'm not afraid, here I am."

I noticed at that point that Smith's lax demeanor was spreading to others. Now perhaps I was feeling the same temptation. Perhaps it was because we sensed the end was actually within reach. Although we did not know what was ahead, the worst appeared to be behind us. We became cocky and brash. Now that we had the upper hand, we felt this mess would soon be over.

I realize that this was symbolic of the Marine Corps. In basic training, we were humbled and humiliated. By the end, we were confident and cocky. Only another banzai attack would bring us down to earth.

I remember a tale we were told in training about a commanding officer who called his troops together and asked for ten volunteers for a very dangerous mission. Ten men immediately stepped forward. The mission was explained in detail, and the men were warned that it was so hazardous that probably only one of the ten would survive. Each of the ten looked at the other nine with pity. Lt. Alex Smith personified that audacious concept.

I managed to reach Lieutenant Baker's platoon but could not locate him. I instructed his squad leader, Glenn Best, to pass the word on to his platoon leader apprising him of the situation and to move in concert with us. Having achieved that, I began the return to my own men. Again those bullets whistled by and kicked up dirt. That return seemed to be the longest I ever ran. Because I was running at the time, I did not feel a Japanese sniper's high-powered bullet cut through the front of my jacket. Had I felt the full impact of the bullet, I'm certain it would have knocked the cockiness out of me and awakened me to the severity of the occasion. Running and jumping from shell hole to shell hole, I arrived at my area, where I saw Sergeant Schisel and Corporal Kizer. I told Sergeant Schisel to withdraw with the next group. It was the last time I spoke to him. A few minutes later I saw him dead—shot through the neck.

Corporal Kizer and I were the last two to go back. I told him we would run to a rock about twenty-five yards away. Just as he reached the rock he was hit and fell to the ground, rolling behind the rock. I jumped next to him only to see that he was hit in the kidney and bleeding badly. He was conscious but in severe pain. I reached over to pull him completely behind the rock, because the Japanese were still shooting at us. As I did so, I felt a very hard blow on my left leg, knocking me down. I clutched my thigh and felt the blood soaking my trousers. I crawled back behind the rock. My leg was completely numb; I couldn't move. I pressed on the artery in my thigh to stop further loss of blood.

Here we were behind that rock, the two of us, useless to each other. Corpsman Young braved the enemy fire and came to take care of both of us. Two litter carriers came to carry Kizer out because his wounds were more serious than mine.

When we landed on Iwo, the scope of my attention had been devoted primarily to the men of my 60-mm mortar platoon. My relationship to others was casual, but with my own men, I got to know and appreciate them personally. In censoring and distributing their mail, one of my duties as

A plasma ward on Iwo Jima. Our medical corpsmen risked their lives under fire to tend to the wounded.

an officer, I was privileged to learn about their families, girlfriends, interests, politics, likes, and dislikes. My relationship with Jerry Kizer, who was not of my original platoon, was less personal. All that changed, however, after the loss of my senior company officers during our first battle. My relationship and responsibility suddenly extended to all of the men from one platoon to the next throughout the company. Thus it was with Cpl. Jerry Kizer. We were wounded together, stranded together, the only two left in the ambush and helpless. These are the ingredients of an indissoluble bond. During our last phase my reliance on Corporal Kizer had grown from casual to deep

Cpl. Jerry Kizer. Wounded and stranded together behind a rock after an ambush in the northern cliffs, we formed an indissoluble tie. Courtesy of Harriet Kizer Bond

dependency. Kizer, in his quiet, unassuming manner, managed to get things done. He was very easygoing but firm. He was sincere and dedicated, and personified the seriousness of purpose instilled in the elite Marines Corps.

The litter carriers told me there was no stretcher for me, and that they would come back. Thoughts of being stranded now entered my mind. I was alone and remembered hearing about the Japanese pulling the wounded and dead Marines of a previous patrol into their caves. With this in the back of my mind, I pulled out my .45 caliber pistol, reloaded my carbine, and laid my ammunition in front of me, ready to use in case the Japanese came out after me. I counted my ammunition, cocked my pistol, took my hand grenades off my belt, and braced myself for what was to come. I wasn't looking forward to this and prayed for a miracle to save me.

It must have been about 1700 (5:00 P.M.) and there was still no sign of rescue. Did they forget me or were they wounded? As I waited, I tossed a handful of dirt from behind the rock to attract the enemy's attention. As I thought, the Japanese fired just to let me know they were still there and had not forgotten me. Now all I could do was wait and ponder, Will I ever get out of here? If not, what will they do to me? Will they come after me right then or wait until it was dark? I didn't think it would ever come to this. I remember thinking of home and my parents and praying, Lord, please help me. My parents already had been notified that my brother, just two days after his nineteenth birthday, had been shot down over Germany. I did not want them to receive more devastating news. I had to think positively and not consume my thoughts with negative possibilities. I would not wait for the enemy to come. I would get out on my own as soon as darkness set in.

I began to massage my leg to gain some feeling, but it remained numb. I continued to rub it anyway. The Japanese knew where I was, but I could not see them. Even if I did, I would not use my ammunition. I had to save it in the event they came after me.

My other option was to wait patiently for darkness and hope that some feeling might return to my leg, then try to crawl back, trusting that my men would recognize me in the dark and hold their fire. Though I realized it was our common practice to shoot at anything or anyone that moved in front of our lines at night, I had no other choice. That was less of a risk than waiting behind that rock for the Japanese to come after me. I made up my mind that if help did not arrive by dark, I was going to crawl back the best I could.

Some twenty or thirty more minutes elapsed and from a distance, and to my rear, I heard Cpl. Bud Krohn, of Hobart, Indiana, our demolitions expert, yelling to me to stay put and that help was coming. Krohn was a constant target to the enemy because they feared his demolitions. Despite his vulnerability, he never showed signs of caution or reluctance to step forward to accomplish his dangerous tasks.

Corporal Krohn came closer, yelled out that he saw me, and asked our replacement captain for help to pull me out. The captain refused, however, because no stretcher was available, and he wouldn't order anyone to certain death. Krohn took it upon himself to help. He stopped two ammunition carriers from another company who were passing through our area and told them that his lieutenant was wounded and helpless behind that rock. He asked for their assistance. They dropped their ammunition and joined him to help me, a stranger. Krohn ran toward me with the two Marines, whom I didn't recognize, all three dodging bullets.

Although I was the officer, Corporal Krohn was definitely in command. He ordered the two "Samaritans" to pull me by my arms as he and others covered our withdrawal. Without a stretcher, they pulled me as I bounced along on my stomach from one hole to another. I could hear the bullets whistling by, and as we moved I thought what easy targets these two rescuers were. I was in a prone position, and consequently less of a target, but they were vulnerable, running in an erect position. If just one of them got hit, all of us would be dead. Only the hand of God protected us as we moved by leaps and bounds. Once out of imminent danger, I turned to thank the two Marines who had risked their lives to help me. But I saw they were already on their way to their unit carrying the ammo cases. I asked Corporal Krohn who they were. He said he did not know. In the years that followed I prayed that God would protect them along with Corporal Krohn and Corpsman Young.

At times it appeared that the only sure way of leaving Iwo Jima alive was to be wounded. Yet, in fighting, one is too preoccupied to think of one's own safety. The fact is, you think even less of your own welfare when it comes to helping a buddy in need. The battle brought out the best in men through their willingness to sacrifice for each other. There were many such heroic deeds on that tiny island.

I remember, while waiting to be moved to the field hospital, Battalion Executive Officer Maj. Donald Hubbard, of Maryland, expressed his concern. He placed a few containers of concentrated brandy into my hands. The brandy was available for medicinal purposes, shock, and cold nights. He told me to have a party wherever I was going. I knew my fighting was over and for that I was relieved. But it was a hollow feeling. Although I was wounded and useless to our men, I felt I was abandoning them.

Chapter 14

Barabbas or Jesus?

On my first day ashore at Iwo, I had noticed a severed hand on the side of the road as we moved up to Airfield No. 1. It must have been blown off at the wrist. It made an impression on me, and throughout the campaign I kept thinking about it.

Now, a couple of weeks later, as I was being evacuated by a medical jeep to the field hospital, we traveled over that same road. For some reason unknown to me, the driver stopped at that same spot. The hand, as I had seen it on the first day, was still there. The incident was a puzzlement, and I drew the driver's attention to it. Was I dreaming, or was the hand real? By his reaction I was assured that this was not my imagination. Though it relieved me to know I was still in command of my sanity, I wondered why the driver had stopped the jeep at that very spot—and just long enough. We continued on to the field hospital, arriving there just as it became dark.

That hand has become etched in my mind. I still see it.

The medics treated me and gave me something to knock me out. It was the first full night of sleep I had had on the island. The next morning I was fed my first solid meal in two weeks. Then they told me I would be flown back to a hospital on Guam.

Just before I was placed on the plane, I realized I was going to leave Iwo Jima forever. I went through my pockets to discard whatever mementos I refused to bring back. I got rid of my combat maps and other material that I felt would be dreadful reminders of the past two weeks. When I put my hand in my left breast pocket, I pulled out the Bible that I had carried throughout the campaign and noticed that the lower corner had been chewed by the bullet that went through my jacket. I also saw that the steel shaving mirror I had used as a bookmark had served to deflect the trajectory of the bullet. Without the Bible or the steel bookmark, that bullet would have gone right through my heart. I ripped my jacket apart and saw that my T-shirt had one long cut across the chest, as though it were slit by a razor. I pulled off my shirt to see what else I might discover. The bullet had come close enough to cut my undershirt but not my skin. I saw that my jacket had two holes, one on the left side where the bullet had entered and one on the right where it had exited.

My first reaction was one of disbelief. Two weeks without significant food and rest, with uninterrupted stress and strain, had left me unable to fully comprehend the meaning of what I was holding in my hand. I examined the Bible, ran my finger through the bullet holes in my combat jacket, and felt the jagged edge of the bullet hole in the steel bookmark. It was just too bewildering. Could the Bible be real? I had heard of a Bible saving someone's life in combat, but somehow I could not associate that blessing with my own unwarranted experience. Obviously, I had not done anything to justify this. Why me? I looked again to see if the Bible was really there. I still did not believe it. I was ashamed to ask someone directly because I thought that my sleepless nights had affected my senses. If this was not real and I told someone, I would be too embarrassed.

Nevertheless, I needed validation. As I was carried on the plane, I conspicuously placed the Bible in view of anyone coming by and waited for a reaction. A corpsman apprached, noticed it, and asked, "Wow, is that yours?" Now I was convinced and grateful to our Lord.

Then I thought of Lieutenant McGinnis. Just before we had departed the USS *Leedstown* to board the landing craft, we had inventoried our equipment to make sure we were

The Bible and the steel shaving mirror that I carried in my left breast pocket saved me from serious injury and possibly death. The page in the Bible was opened to the date May 16, the exact date of my arrival in San Francisco. John A Gibson, Jr. *Bradenton Herald*

carrying only what we would need on the island. I had pushed my shaving equipment aside with other unnecessary items. McGinnis had said jokingly, "Why don't you put that steel shaving mirror in the Bible that you always carry; it might save your life." I placed the mirror in the Bible as he suggested but never thought it would serve that purpose. I said, "It fits perfectly; I needed a bookmark anyway."

All pages of the Bible are dated, each page relating to a specific theme from the New Testament. I had randomly placed the steel mirror as a bookmark without looking at the date on that page—May 16. The impact of the bullet had forced the mirror to break the binding, causing the Bible to fall open at that particular page. After being hospitalized on Guam, I was transferred to the naval hospital on Hawaii and eventually back to the States. The hospital ship that brought me back to the States arrived at the Golden Gate Bridge in San Francisco on May 16, the exact date on the page at which I had randomly placed the mirror back in February. The theme of that dated page is "Barabbas or Jesus?" Choose one.

Chapter 15

Our New Neighbors

Because the navy hospitals in the Marianas were occupied to capacity, Iwo's wounded were taken to the army hospital on Guam. The care I received there was outstanding. Convalescing was enhanced by the efficient and cooperative staff.

But the serenity of this safe haven was interrupted one night as we were awakened abruptly by a loud explosion. My first impulse was to duck for cover. For a moment I thought we were back on Iwo. The nurses informed us that the ammunition depot had blown up. A few days later they said that one of our planes had exploded as the pilot was attempting to land.

After a couple of weeks on Guam, we were placed on a hospital ship to take us to the naval hospital in Hawaii. On Easter Sunday morning, April 1, 1945, the public address system aboard the ship announced the following, "[T]he combined forces of the U.S. Marines and Army landed on Okinawa." There was dead silence. Sudden stillness prevailed throughout the ship. Except for the crew, everyone aboard was a wounded survivor of Iwo Jima.

Just weeks before, we ourselves had been engaged in combat. The horror of battle was still fresh in our minds and our bones; our feelings and prayers for our comrades were in our hearts.

We were elated over the fact we were heading stateside and that we were spared the risk of future combat, at least for the immediate future. At the same time, many of us expressed a deep sense of support and loyalty for our brothers in arms, along with a strong feeling of guilt that we were not able to turn the ship around to help them.

A dead Japanese soldier amid boxes from his expended ammunition. The horror of war stayed fresh in our minds and our bones for years to come. Author's collection

I learned quickly the inaccuracy of the premise that one gives up one's life for one's country. It serves no purpose to give your life in combat. One serves one's comrades and one's country best by remaining alive to continue the pursuit. No one I saw was willing to die. The truth is that life was snatched from them; it was not given.

One may risk one's life attempting to save a wounded buddy while under heavy enemy fire or to salvage a potentially desperate situation. In attempting to rescue someone, one does not plan to become a casualty oneself. One is not giving one's life. One is certainly aware of the risk without the intention of giving one's life. Otherwise, one is committing suicide and that's best left for the enemy.

On Hawaii, I was taken to the naval hospital in Aeia Heights, Honolulu, were I was placed in a hospital barrack. Located nearby was another barrack that was surrounded by two barbed wire fences, one inside the other, and guarded by military police. This barrack housed "special guests," wounded Japanese who had been captured on Iwo. The security measures were designed not only to keep the POWs from escaping, but also to protect them against Marines who had to be restrained from trying to attack the guarded barrack. A short time ago we had been in combat trying to kill each other. Now the enemy was receiving medical care from our doctors and was protected by our own military police. It was conceivable that we might have met on Iwo through each other's rifle sights. Now we could see them receiving blood plasma donated by American citizens and intended for the use of our own wounded. How could a few days make all the difference?

I had to pass the prisoner's barrack on the way to the mess hall. It didn't take long before I began to recognize some of the faces as they peered through the windows, our eyes meeting through that barbed wire. Over a period of time, a faint smile or a reluctant gesture of acceptance passed between us. Eventually, this recognition was manifested in a distant and deliberate wave of the hand. Within days, our means of communication had changed from rifles and bullets to smiles and waves. I thought that, after all, they as individuals did not want the war any more than we did; they merely had followed orders. Though there was no exchange of words, I felt that each of us, through silent communication, was acknowledging that the other was also human. Perhaps we sensed a spark of hope for the future along with a measure of mercy for the enemy.

Chapter 16

Peace

The homebound hospital ship arrived in San Francisco on May 16, 1945. The sight of the Golden Gate Bridge was a glorious experience. I had seen it before, but never before did it take my breath away.

After a few days of processing at a hospital, the wounded were transported to a train that would drop us off at locations of hospitals closer to our homes. The train was filled exclusively with wounded servicemen. We had medical care second to none. I arrived at my home in Jersey City with orders to report to St. Albans Navy Hospital in Long Island, New York. I had phoned my parents from San Francisco, and again from Chicago, where the train had stopped to change engines and crew. As I entered my house, the scene was as expected—one of joy mixed with tears. The joy came to an end the next morning, however, when my mother informed me that the Army Air Force had notified her and my father that my brother's status of "missing in action" had been changed to "killed in action."

On August 14, 1945, I was on limited duty stationed at the Marine barracks at the Brooklyn Navy Yard. Returning from an assignment in the vicinity of Times Square, I heard the news that Japan had surrendered. The war was over! People were shouting and horns were blowing. Delirious with the news of victory, everyone seemed to go wild. Crowds were greeting each other, strangers were hugging and kissing strangers. The air raid sirens were blasting continuously to mark the end of an era and hopefully the beginning of a better one.

Although the news had been anticipated, we had had to wait for it a few days. When it arrived, the celebration was spontaneous. I remember being somewhat numb. My first reaction was "It's over—that's great! That means we don't have to fight on the Japanese homeland, and the troops are coming home." Then I thought of those who were not coming home, the men I knew and those I did not know. Foremost in my mind was my kid brother, Eddie, who was shot down over Germany. We wouldn't see him again.

I felt that I didn't belong in the midst of this celebration, that I should be home with my parents. I brushed away a few tears and headed for the subway to take me home to Jersey City. As I reached the stairway to the tracks, throngs of people were coming up to join in the excitement. I was probably the only one leaving it, and had to fight my way through the thundering herd.

When I finally reached home, mixed with feelings of joy and pain, my parents and I consoled each other. They didn't say it, but I read it in their eyes. "We lost Eddie, you're home, your brother Mario, and your brother-in-law Charles should soon be home."

Part 6

Nightmare in Hell

Chapter 17

Men of Uncommon Valor

The following stories are by and about the men who fought on Iwo Jima. As prime witnesses, it is our duty to augment the official records of the battle with the personal and human aspects of combat.

Sergeants Three: Henry, Shorter, Schisel

During my time on Iwo Jima I had three different sergeants in my command. When we landed, I was in charge of the company's 60-mm mortars and Sgt. James Henry of Nebraska was my noncommissioned officer (NCO). On the second day, after we lost five of the seven officers, I also had charge of the company's machine guns and Sgt. Harvey Shorter was the NCO. On the fourth day, I was assigned a rifle platoon. The NCO of that platoon was Sgt. Gordon Schisel. Each one of the sergeants was tops in his respective function. Each was killed.

I knew Sergeant Henry best. While on Guam, he was second in command of the mortar section. We had ongoing discussions concerning our men and the methods of training. As it should be, the lieutenant and his NCO are the two closest men in the platoon. Such was the case with us. I had full confidence in Sergeant Henry's ability. Whenever something was expected of him, I always knew it would be accomplished. We were close in friendship and in our thinking.

Sergeant Henry was in his late twenties, easy going, friendly, and the owner of a perpetual smile. He lived on a farm in Nebraska, and all the money he earned in the Marine Corps was put aside for additions to his farm back home. On the ship to Iwo, he told me that his older brother was holding a few hundred acres of land until his return home. Although I was never too interested in farming, I liked to listen to Sergeant Henry proudly talk about his Nebraska land and his future plans.

Sergeant Henry and I occupied the same foxholes for those first few nights on Iwo. When I was reassigned to a rifle platoon, he came with me as forward observer for the 60-mm mortars. He was nearby at all times. In the event my platoon came across good mortar targets, he would be there as our forward observer to direct his rapid and accurate fire. It was standard practice for men sharing a foxhole to divide the security watch. Henry and I alternated being awake two hours at a time until dawn. A keen observer and always alert, Sergeant Henry was the best. One night while he was on watch he awakened me and whispered that he thought the Japanese were crawling around our foxholes. I listened and looked, then disagreed. Later we heard grenades going off. The Japanese had actually crawled into our area and dropped grenades into our foxholes. The next morning I noticed an enemy grenade in our foxhole. Fortunately, it was a dud that had failed to detonate.

On the morning of March 6, Sergeant Henry was standing next to me zeroing in his mortar rounds while I was talking to the colonel via walkie-talkie. Suddenly I felt his body hit me from the rear—like being clipped in a football game. At first I didn't understand what had happened. I thought he had lost his footing until I realized that he had been shot and had fallen against me. I picked myself up on my hands and knees and noticed that he had been hit in the head. The bullet had penetrated his helmet, gone right through his temple and out the back of his head. He was unconscious, rolling over, twisting, turning, and moaning. Corpsman Young was nearby and came immediately. I'll never forget the expression on Sergeant Henry's face as he was dying. Though he was unconscious, his eyes were open. He was staring pitiably at me as I held him and Doc Young worked on him. By then I had seen many dead and wounded, but none affected me as much as the sight of Sergeant Henry dying in my arms. Doc Young made a valiant, though futile, effort to hold life in him long enough for the doctors aboard ship to attempt to save him. He was carried back to the battalion aid station, where he died.

The second sergeant under my command was Harvey Shorter. I didn't know him as well as I knew Sergeant Henry, but I was sure he was a good Marine and was master of his machine guns. One time Shorter removed his helmet as shells landed nearby. After the shelling ceased, I went to that sector of the line to assess the casualties. When I reached Shorter, he showed me how the last one came as close to him as he ever wanted. A piece of shrapnel had cut through his hair. There was a portion of his head that became a bald spot; the butt of later humor, even at times as serious as these.

Several days later I was informed that Sergeant Shorter was following Lt. Ken Thompson's platoon with his section of machine guns. Thompson's platoon encountered heavy

Left to right, K Company Sgt. Harvey Shorter, with Sgts. Lionel Siefken, Charles McCain, and Jim Boman. Courtesy of Bill Bryant

fire. While placing his guns to support Thompson's men, Sergeant Shorter was shot and killed by enemy gunfire.

Gordon Schisel was the third sergeant under my command as I was assigned to the Second Rifle Platoon. He was in his early twenties, good-looking, cooperative, intelligent, unafraid of the enemy, anxious to take charge of small patrols, most considerate of those under him, a hard worker, likeable, and very dependable.

I always felt Sergeant Schisel would make a good officer. He never needed a picture to explain what had to be done. He often suggested means that proved most helpful to me. Most of the nights after I took over the Second Platoon I had Sergeant Schisel and Doc Young dig their foxholes near mine. In that way the second-in-command was always near enough to enable me to pass on anything of importance, and naturally the corpsman was close and ready to be summoned to a casualty anytime he was needed.

In the daytime, however, while we attacked the enemy, Sergeant Schisel either took charge of a section of the platoon or he would bring up the rear of the platoon. For eleven days on Iwo, until he was killed, we worked well as a team, coordinating the movement of our command.

It was certainly more than good fortune to have shared the experiences of these extraordinary, fine sergeants.

Felix Tschida

Probably the most amazing and astounding experience occurring to any individual on Iwo Jima must be attributed to Pfc. Felix Tschida, of St. Paul, Minnesota.

Tschida and a fellow Marine were scouts of their platoon on a day when our forces had already taken the southern half of Iwo Jima. The scout's function is to precede the main body of the platoon to detect any evidence of the enemy by drawing their fire and revealing their position. It is actually a security measure to prevent the majority of the unit from becoming ambushed. It is a dangerous function, but a necessary one, whose premise is based upon sacrificing a few for the safety of many.

Tschida and his partner were moving toward the unseen enemy forces when rifle shots whistled by. The other scout evaded the enemy's bullets, and from the rock behind which he took refuge he was able to see that Tschida was badly hit. Blood was flowing from his motionless body. The scout's reaction was normal under such conditions: creeping and crawling back to his platoon he reported what had happened and the enemy's location. He explained that Tschida was hit, bleeding badly, and appeared to be dead. Just then the Japanese poured a barrage of shells into the platoon area to discourage an oncoming attack. Their fire continued intermittently for a few hours. Anyone's guess was that Tschida certainly must have died by this time.

Tschida, however, was not yet dead. He was hit in the neck, one bullet severing his vocal cord, another penetrating his lung. The impact of the bullets knocked him unconscious. He lay there for a few hours until dusk ushered in the darkness of night. After several hours he came to, but did not know what had happened—except that he could not speak. He felt weak and his jacket was soaked with blood. He did not know if his platoon had taken the hill to the front. There was no sign of anyone else from his outfit—no sign of anyone at all—and it was night. Whenever he tried to move, a few more enemy bullets flew by. That meant the Japanese knew his location and still held the hill. His platoon's attack must have been repelled. All that night he kept falling unconscious and "coming to," only to realize his hopeless predicament.

At dawn more artillery shells were hitting the hill. It was apparent now that the Japanese were still in control of the hill, that we were giving preparatory artillery fire to support another attack, and that Tschida was in the middle of the shooting. Whenever he raised himself to see what was going on, the Japanese would let him know he was still being observed. The firing would stop, then start heavier than before. The entire day passed and Tschida was in the same place, getting weaker, thirstier, and hungrier as time went by. He had already consumed his canteen of water and had only a portion of his K ration in his pack.

Having endured his second day out there, he began his second long night. (Nothing ever seemed as unending as one night on Iwo Jima.) Wounded, with loss of blood, infection setting in, lack of food and water, fatigue, unable to move, psychologically insecure—this was Tschida's predicament. He could have accepted the circumstances and just regarded himself as a dead Marine, but not Tschida; he would not quit.

He thought of setting out his canteen cup and mess gear so that he might have drinking water if it rained. More artillery, more illuminating shells, more machine gun bursts, more high-powered rifle shots, but no rain. It all seemed so bizarre. Perhaps he would wake up to find that this was only a bad dream. But a few close shells, bursts, or a ricochet was sufficient for him to understand that it was not a bad dream but the most serious business in the world. One of the close bursts riddled his canteen cup full of holes. Oh well, it made no difference. It did not rain that night anyway. He had now gone through his second torturous night. He still existed—but barely.

It was the beginning of the third day, and there was still no sign of Marine occupancy of the hill. There was not much to look forward to—not much hope of rescue. The conditions remained the same on that day except for the fact that Tschida was weaker. Then the third night commenced. The Japanese knew where Tschida was and that he was wounded. Tschida didn't understand why they did not come out to capture him. He was not going to try his luck another night. He was determined not to wait there any longer. He was going to force himself to try crawling back to his lines. The enemy had less chance of seeing him move in the night. It had to be that night because he might not have the strength to live to the next one.

From the sounds of the firing, he estimated the distance back to his platoon. He started to crawl, creep, and roll, feeling the pain as he moved. It took a few hours to move half the distance. All of a sudden an illuminating shell lit up above him. (We used these shells to brighten the sky in defense against sneak night attacks.) His buddies on the line saw Tschida move, and two machine gunners, thinking he was a Japanese soldier infiltrating the Marine position, opened fire on him. He could not shout who he really was, as his vocal cord had been severed. He dropped into a shell crater and waited. Since he couldn't yell to his comrades, he took his helmet off and moved it over his head. As he had hoped, it made those trigger-happy leathernecks on the line a bit cautious, and they held their fire. He slowly raised himself out of the crater and continued to crawl toward the line. Finally, his buddies recognized him; they came out to him and pulled him back to the lines. He passed out again but awoke to find himself being treated by a doctor. He heard someone say that bullets had torn his cartridge belt. He passed out again. A chaplain came to talk to him. Since the doctors saw no hope for his survival, the priest rendered the last rites and his dog tag was cut from his chain to be sent to headquarters for notification of next of kin.

Upon waking the next morning, he felt a cover over his entire body. Slowly, with what little life remained, he worked the blanket down over his face and noticed he was in a tent with others who also were covered with blankets or ponchos. He realized he was in an improvised morgue, but could not speak to anyone that a mistake had been made. As litter carriers carrying the dead came in, he blinked his eyes and feebly moved his head to attract their attention in order to let them know that he was still alive. Half-scared, the men panicked and ran out to summon help. A medic arrived to inject more morphine into Tschida's arm, putting him to sleep. This time he had a restful sleep and awoke aboard a hospital ship.

But all his problems were not in the past. His wife had received a telegram from the War Department that he had been killed in action. In the meantime, aboard ship, Tschida asked me to write to his wife that he was wounded but alive. I wrote it in the first person as he requested and signed his name. His wife notified the authorities that she had received a letter, dated subsequent to the alleged date of his death, and that he was indeed alive. They requested the letter and responded that the handwriting was not that of her husband. It was weeks before the discrepancy was resolved.

Pfc. Felix Tschida did not receive a medal for his courage, nor will many others who deserve them. But his award for that which he so well exemplified on those lonely, helpless, and endless nights was the ultimate one: that of life itself, presented by God.

Joe D'Amico

Pfc. Joe D'Amico, from Baltimore, Maryland, joined our company on Guam a couple of months before we left for Iwo Jima. D'Amico was not yet twenty years of age. He was married and had a child. We talked a lot about places we both knew in Maryland and became good friends. As battalion insurance officer it was my job, among other duties, to acquaint all new men with the provisions of government life insurance. D'Amico didn't believe in insurance. He was afraid it would jinx him and continued to resist my plea. But just before leaving Guam he finally agreed to the small monthly deduction so that his family would be covered in the event that he was killed.

Not long after we landed on Iwo Jima, D'Amico was taken back to our transport because of battle stress. He was released a few days later and rejoined us. As the battle progressed our numbers dwindled so I got to know him better. One night, as we shared the same foxhole, a Japanese soldier crawled up to us and dropped a grenade on us. D'Amico picked it up and threw it right back. On another occasion we were involved in an exchange of fire with the enemy when the rifle was shot right out of D'Amico's arm. The bullet hit the butt of his rifle and passed between his shoulder and head, just missing him. He was astonished. "Wow, was that close," he laughed.

The night before I was wounded, D'Amico and I had just dug in when we repelled several small banzai attacks. In these suicide attacks the Japanese always announced their charge by yelling patriotic phrases at the top of their lungs. They came charging, waving swords, and running straight at us. At times they overwhelmed us by their great numbers. As one of these attacks subsided, D'Amico fired some shots at a Japanese soldier who was hit but still moving just ten yards or so from our foxhole. I could see that he had hit the man in his leg. Several minutes later that same Japanese, from the prone position, tossed a grenade at us. The grenade missed us, and we both fired at him again. We knew we hit him because his body bounced from the impact of our bullets. He played dead again and sometime later raised himself once more to fire at us. Again we returned the fire. We carefully observed him throughout the night to be sure he was, indeed, dead. Many Japanese did not die by a single shot or two.

At daybreak we went through the dead man's belongings, a standard procedure, searching for possible valuable military information. D'Amico removed two Japanese flags from this fellow who had refused to die. He asked me for permission to keep the flags as souvenirs. One of the flags was wrapped around the man's waist and had a stain of blood from where he had been hit the previous night. I told D'Amico to keep the flags; he offered one to me. Although I wanted one, I refused it to set the example against collecting souvenirs, which was taboo on Iwo.

The next day D'Amico was with me on my last patrol. He came to me after I'd been wounded and was ready to depart to the hospital, placed the blood-stained flag in my hands, and said, "I know you want it. This was from the guy who tried to kill us last night. You won't have another chance to get one of these. I will." I accepted his gift graciously. He then requested that if I got home before he did, "please visit my family and hug my kid." He was killed a few days later and I fulfilled his request.

Bob Roney

Lt. Bob Roney, of Independence, Missouri, was hit on the first day while leading his platoon in the attack on Airfield No. 2. He remembers approaching the rim of a large shell crater when an enemy shell landed nearby, knocking him unconscious and into the crater. He was temporarily blinded and evacuated to Guam, then to the naval hospital at Aeia Heights, Honolulu, where he underwent the first of many surgeries to remove volcanic ash from his eyes.

Karl J. Schmidt

Cpl. Karl J. Schmidt, of Peoria, Illinois, was wounded twice on Guam. He was hospitalized, recovering from his wounds and released in time to rejoin his outfit, Ninth Marines, Third Division. He recalls he didn't have time to unpack his gear. The next day, "We shipped out for Iwo."

Schmidt remembers witnessing a U.S. dive bomber breaking in two and plunging into the sea and others going down in flames from Japanese antiaircraft guns.

He was assigned to carry ammunition to the rifle companies on the front line and to carry the dead and wounded off the battlefield. "There were so many dead, row after row of dead Marines. They had to be pushed by a bulldozer into a shallow ditch and covered until the island was secured for proper burial.

"Snipers were shooting at us even while driving my jeep carrying dead Marines. The Japanese ambushed a marked ambulance jeep, killing the two wounded in it and the two medical corpsmen. There was no way to move without getting shot at.

"I was carrying ammunition across Airfield No. 2. When I got halfway across, a machine gun opened up on me. I saw a shell hole and jumped in. I waited and three times I raised my head to check if it was safe, and each time, the machine gunner fired at me. I waited and all of a sudden it got very dark and started to rain very heavy. I got up, left the ammo in the shell hole and ran back to my unit.

"Another time I came across a cook's supply tent when I heard a shot. I got down next to a row of boxes for protection when I heard another shot whiz by. I felt something on my helmet. The bullet hit about eight inches above my head, making a hole in a can of tomato juice that poured down on me. For a moment I thought I was bleeding.

"The next day I came by a knocked-out antiaircraft bunker. I looked in to check it out and saw dead Japanese on the floor. I walked down some steps and noticed one-hundred-pound sacks piled up and rows of canned goods. I opened a can and saw fish heads with eyes looking at me. I used my knife to cut one of the sacks and rice poured out—got out of there in a hurry. I was hungry, but no thank you.

"I was near Airfield No. 2 when a disabled American plane on the way back from bombing Japan made an emergency landing. It was badly shot up. Even though the fighting was still going on, that plane and many others that would not have made it back to Saipan were saved by landing on Iwo.

"When the Ninth Marines reached the north end, my buddy and I were carrying ammo to one of the companies on the front line. A Marine from K Company called out to us that his lieutenant was wounded and stranded out there and that no stretcher was left to get him out. He needed help, so we dropped our ammo boxes and went out for him. Without a stretcher, we had to pull him out by the arms. They were firing at us, but we got him out of there. I didn't know who he was; we picked up our ammo and headed on our way. We delivered the ammo and on the way back we ran into some Japs. My buddy was killed. I don't know how I got back. I guess I was lucky at that time."

Schmidt was hit by shrapnel on the eighteenth day of Iwo and taken to a temporary aid station to await treatment. Enemy shells landed next to his tent. "The barrage was so heavy and continuous that I couldn't take it any longer. I must have passed out or been unconscious. The next thing I knew I was on a hospital ship."

Fifty years after Iwo, a friend gave Schmidt a copy of the Associated Press release in which I described how I was wounded, unable to move, and stranded between the enemy and our lines. The article relayed how after all hope of survival was exhausted, two Marines, unknown to me, ran to me and in full view of the enemy, in the midst of gunfire, carried me over the open field to safety; that when I turned to thank them, they had already left to rejoin their own unit; and that I did not know their names, but in my prayers, had never forgotten them.

Schmidt recognized the incident. He and his buddy were the two unidentified Samaritans who risked their own lives to come to my rescue.

I recently spoke with him. He recalled the episode in detail. I finally was able to thank him by phone—if not in person.

Karl Schmidt, *left,* and entertainer Jack Benny in a hospital. Fifty years after Iwo, Karl Schmidt received the Associated Press release in which I described how I was wounded, stranded between the enemy and our lines, and rescued by two Marines who were unknown to me. Schmidt recognized the incident. He and his buddy were the two unidentified Samaritans. Courtesy of Karl Schmidt

On Iwo we were surrounded by Angels of Death. We also had Angels of Life. Karl Schmidt was one of them.

Royce K. Beavers

Royce K. Beavers, of Lockport, Illinois, was a machine gunner in K Company. After reaching Airfield No. 2, we advanced to an open area and up a rise, where we established our next line. Beavers and James Griffen noticed several Japanese moving about one hundred yards to their front. Beavers said, "We stared at each other, then decided to fire a few quick bursts as a courtesy call." It was nothing more than a calling card, merely to announce our presence. They responded with a 75- or 77-mm howitzer, probably making a statement, "OK, we see you, too!" That was the end of the exchange for the moment. Each side deferred to a later encounter. "They could have wiped us out with their superior firepower at that time. I don't know why they didn't," stated Beavers.

That night we received more replacements. One was assigned to Beavers's squad. At dusk, Beavers explained to the young, inexperienced Marine that they would take turns on watch throughout the night. Beavers took the first watch, then the replacement relieved him. Several hours passed. Beavers woke up on his own and asked the young Marine, "Why didn't you wake me at the end of the hour instead of letting me sleep all this time?" The replacement replied, "I tried to, but every time you kept cussing me out. I didn't want to bother you anymore." He stayed on watch all that time, but he learned better in a few days.

Dave Thompson

Lt. Dave Thompson, from Oregon, appeared much younger than his twenty-five years. He had blond, curly hair; he was good-looking, sincere, dedicated, and good-natured. He had attended the University of Hawaii. He was in charge of the Third Platoon. We called him "Cold Steel" to symbolize his determination and aggressive leadership. However, to me the most striking feature about him was his strong belief in tolerance for all mankind. Dave Thompson was the personification of the golden rule. In combat, however, he was a furious fighter and a respected leader, but he would become personally offended if anyone spoke in derogatory terms against any minority group. His generosity extended to my possessions as well as his own on one particular occasion. While we were training on Guam, he had run out of his beer rations, so he gave away my rations to passersby who were thirsty. He justified it to me by saying, "I knew you wouldn't have deprived them." He also knew I could not become angry with him.

When Captain Crawford and Lieutenant McGinnis were hit, Thompson was in command of our company. His command, however, was short lived. Within minutes he was hit by a Japanese shell, causing the loss of his left leg.

I saw him weeks later at the hospital in Hawaii. He never complained about his misfortune. A hospital support group came to console and prepare him psychologically for the future. He abruptly interrupted them and told them he had definite, positive plans to get an artificial leg and would walk, dance, and run again. Then he politely excused them. Sometime later, he was fitted with a temporary leg. He had become accustomed to it by walking several hours a day without the help of a crutch. I remember one day we decided to hitchhike from the hospital to Honolulu. Having attended the University of Hawaii prior to the war, he wanted to show me around. I was walking with a cane, and he decided to dismantle his artificial leg and use his two crutches. I asked him why he was removing the artificial leg and reminded him that the doctors ordered him to wear it constantly. He explained humorously as he was pinning the trouser leg to his waist, "We'll get a ride much faster this way," and we did!

Thompson showed me the high spots of the city and then we had dinner. Later, he took me to a meeting of about twenty people. I'm certain he had planned this but kept it a secret from me. It turned out to be a labor rally of the International Longshoremen and Warehousemen Union (ILWU), raising their voices against the injustices of the era. Of course, Thompson was vocal for the cause.

After the war Thompson remained in Hawaii and married his sweetheart, his inspiration, Mitsue. He was active in the ILWU, serving as director of education for the organization for thirty-three years, up to his untimely death.

John Silva

Cpl. John Silva, of Long Island, New York, was in my platoon when we left San Diego, California, for the Guam campaign. Silva, a handsome, former male model, was a machine gun squad leader. He was competent, modest, and cheerful. He had married a lovely model who worked with him in New York City. He carried her picture in his wallet and proudly talked a great deal about her and the times they spent at Martha's Vineyard. I was sorry to learn he was assigned to another battalion of the Ninth Marine Regiment after the Guam campaign. He was killed on Iwo.

Troy Young, Bud Krohn, Joe Simone

The bravery displayed by Corpsman Troy Young, Cpl. Bud Krohn, and Cpl. Joe Simone led me to write detailed accounts of their actions and strongly recommend to my superiors that they each be duly recognized for military honors. In a campaign characterized by Adm. Chester W. Nimitz as where "uncommon valor was a common virtue," these three men stood high above the rest of us.

After the war, while I was stationed at the Brooklyn Navy Yard, I met Colonel Boehm and asked him if my recommendation for honors for these three men had been approved. He told me that he had endorsed my letters and had passed them on for further action. However, he led me to believe that with the war at an end, the need for awarding medals had diminished. Sadly, the honors were never granted.

There were countless others whose deeds are noteworthy and others whose events were unrecorded only because what they did was not witnessed or carried back to others. For this reason, many incidents remain vague at best. I consider it our loss that we have been deprived of their contribution to the cause. Although I don't know many of the details, I do remember them as great men of the Corps.

Ralph Rainbow and Stanley Araujo

Ralph Rainbow, bazooka man, and Stanley Araujo, the captain's runner, were American Indians. All of us in K Company were very proud to serve with them. Both were wounded.

Lewis Springer, Peter Morse, and William Kellogg

As we were preparing to take off for the attack on Airfield No. 2, the Japanese must have had an inkling of our timing. They hit us with a tremendous barrage of their big mortars. When the firing slowed down and we were ready to go, I checked my platoon to give them the signal to attack. I then saw that one of the enemy shells had made a direct hit, wiping out one of my 60-mm mortar squad and killing Lewis Springer, Peter Morse, and William Kellogg. They were killed instantly. All three represented the best of America's youth.

Willie Chustz

Willie Chustz, of Baton Rouge, Louisiana, was wounded on Bougainville and twice on Guam. Just prior to Iwo he was selected to return to the States on the point system. Instead of taking his leave, he passed it on to his brother,

Benny, who was also in K Company. Willie landed on Iwo with us and was wounded for the fourth time, losing his leg.

Angelo "Bert" Bertelli

Lt. Angelo "Bert" Bertelli is a Notre Dame football legend. He won the coveted Heisman Trophy in his senior year and was twice selected for the All-American Team.

We met in boot camp and were assigned to our tents in alphabetical order. This resulted in our being close throughout basic training. We survived that ordeal and went on together through candidates school, reserve officers training, and training with our troops as second lieutenants. We were placed in the same replacement group for overseas.

Two of our classmates, Doug Boyd and Dom Grasso, also landed in the same replacement group. The four of us left for Camp Pendleton, California, for overseas assignment. When we checked into the adjutant's office, we were told there was a transport sailing out in three days and another in three weeks. He asked which we preferred. In unison we selected the first group. He said, "That's good. If you picked the other, I would have placed you in the first group regardless."

We were assigned to troop units that first day and were told the entire replacement group of more than two thousand men had a forty-eight-hour leave. We had to report back by 0700 (7:00 A.M.) on the third day ready to ship overseas. I thought that a forty-eight-hour leave was a mistake—some of the men, overindulging in their last fling before going overseas, might miss the deadline. I doubted that two thousand men would make it back in time. I was so convinced that I offered to wager five dollars to anyone who would accept the challenge. Bertelli did.

After the forty-eight hours expired, we assembled in camp and were driven to the dock. As we boarded the ship, the Marine band played, "I Wonder Who's Kissing Her Now." The California coastline was still in sight when we learned that not only did all of the troops make roll call, but we also had six stowaways onboard.

Bertelli went to a staff position in regimental headquarters; Boyd, Grasso, and I went to rifle companies. After the Guam campaign we trained for Iwo.

When frontline officer casualties ran high on Iwo Jima, battalion and regimental officers were called on to fill the gaps at the front. On the second day, Dom Grasso was

Lt. Angelo "Bert" Bertelli is a Notre Dame football legend. He won the coveted Heisman Trophy in his senior year and was twice selected for the All-American Team. We met in boot camp and went through basic training, candidates school, reserve officers training, and training with our troops as second lieutenants. We eventually were placed in the same replacement group for overseas. Courtesy of Jill Bertelli

killed leading his platoon. Bert Bertelli was called upon to lead Grasso's men, and he did so with distinction for the balance of the campaign. Doug Boyd was twice wounded.

Bertelli experienced a close call when an enemy mortar exploded nearby, killing a medical corpsman next to him. On another occasion, he tossed a grenade into an enemy bunker. To his amazement, the grenade was thrown back at him. They eventually subdued the bunker's occupants. He recalls the most agonizing cry from a Marine who was hit by a napalm bomb, which burned through his clothing and flesh. The bomb was meant for the enemy attacking our position, but it fell on our lines. "The pain is greater when hit by friendly fire," Bertelli said. "You expect to be hit by the enemy, but not by your own forces."

Harry Jones

Lt. Harry Jones of I Company was sent from Guam to Hawaii for an appendectomy just a few weeks before we embarked for Iwo Jima. The day before we left the harbor at Guam, Jones walked into the wardroom aboard the USS *Leedstown* carrying his combat equipment. My first reaction, since he came back so quickly, was that he did not have the surgery. However, we found out that he did have the operation and that he had asked the doctors for permission to return to the battalion in time to be with his troops for the next campaign. The hospital fitted Jones with a special belt, which he wore to protect his incision. Harry Jones, of Tennessee, was killed the first day ashore.

Ken Jackson

Sgt. Ken Jackson was a scout radioman with a forward observer unit. His function was to direct support of the 105-mm howitzers for advancing infantrymen.

He remembers that two of the six Higgins landing boats were blown up as they reached the beach by Japanese 5-inch shells. Later in the battle for Hill 382, "We took the hill five times only to be knocked back each time. On the sixth attempt, led by G Company Commander Capt. Joseph McCarthy of the Twenty-fourth Marine Regiment, we were able to maintain control of the hill. Joe McCarthy received the Medal of Honor."

Many haunting incidents are etched in Jackson's mind. His most vivid is the final gasp of a young Marine who was sharing his foxhole and shot in the chest calling the words, "Mother, Mother."

Joe Graziano

Sgt. Joe Graziano, of Madison, New Jersey, enlisted in the Marine Corps early in the war. He and three of his buddies decided to join as a group, but only Graziano's parents agreed to his enlistment. The others waited to be drafted.

Graziano was in charge of a rescue team, carrying the wounded to medical aid stations on the beach for treatment of minor injuries or to a hospital ship for the more seriously wounded. He remembers that the great number of wounded caused the hospital ships to reach their capacity sooner than anticipated. Other ships had to be used as improvised hospital quarters. Japanese planes attacked his ship. A torpedo hit a transport ship next to his, splitting it in two. Flying fragments hit some of the wounded on his ship. The same planes then struck rows of stretchers of wounded on the shore awaiting evacuation.

Pete Hill

Sgt. Pete Hill, of Madison, Wisconsin, was in K Company since its formation. Iwo Jima was his third landing. He remembers, "As a reserve unit, the landing for us was not too bad, except for the many dead of both sides we had to dodge to reach our position. The flag on Suribachi was a good sight, but Iwo was an ugly looking place."

Hill was on Iwo a week when he was wounded. "One day of combat on that island is more than enough to last a lifetime," he recalls. "On the second day ashore we were dug in on the reverse side of a knoll. I left with a few others to pick up more ammunition. When we returned there, three of our company were killed a few feet from our foxhole. We were told a shell had hit shortly after we left.

"On the second day, Sergeant Ed Causino was put in charge of his platoon to replace his wounded lieutenant. Lieutenants on Iwo were becoming scarce. We were getting ready to push ahead and Causino was giving his men details for the attack. Then to boost their morale, he told them that an ice cream factory had been built on Guam and as soon as we finished here we were going back to take it over. Captain Crawford was standing a few feet from us listening with a big smile on his face. We went into the assault. That's when Crawford was killed.

"On March 1, I was carrying a box of ammo and was hit. The bullet pierced my helmet on the left side, went around the back, and exited through the right side. I dropped to my knees and removed my helmet. I felt my head to see if it was still there; the only damage was two holes in my helmet and the loss of some of my hair.

"On the next day, I was hit by shrapnel in my right arm. I was in a foxhole, my arm stretched out over the side, when a shell landed near us and got me. I was evacuated and hospitalized for a few months. I remember all the guys. You get close to them in a situation like that, but forget some of the details."

Don Clingenpeel, James Taylor, and Lee Kraft

Cpl. Donald Clingenpeel, of Mystic, Connecticut, remembers crossing Airfield No. 2, "seeing many of my buddies getting hit. I was blasted and ended up on hospital ship USS *Solace*. I rejoined K Company on Guam after the Iwo campaign."

Cpl. James Taylor and Cpl. Lee Kraft, members of the same machine gun squad of K Company, made the landings on Bougainville, Guam, and Iwo Jima. On about D plus seven, on Airfield No. 2, they were in their foxhole and on the alert. During a counterattack a Japanese soldier managed to close in on their emplacement and blew himself to pieces with a grenade in an attempt to take Taylor and Kraft along with him. The man fell on the machine gun. Taylor and Kraft were wounded and knocked unconscious. They regained their consciousness aboard a hospital ship a couple of days later.

Taylor admits, "Iwo was a hell on earth. I feel fortunate to have come through all three campaigns and still be alive."

Chapter 18

Reflections

The following recollections, impressions, reflections, and flashbacks are permanently rooted in my memory and nurtured by the passing of time. I'm certain others harbor the same sensations. Such remembrances are inevitable. They remain sharp and vivid despite the passing years.

It's a little known fact that there were three flag raisings on Iwo Jima.

At 0900 (9:00 A.M.) on February 23, 1945, a reconnaissance patrol climbed to the top of Mt. Suribachi. Cpl. Charles Lindberg, of Richfield, Minnesota, carrying his seventy-two-pound flame thrower, was one of the patrol. His function was to eliminate enemy fire from pillboxes along the journey to the top. They reached the summit at 10:30, with minimum resistance.

1st Lt. Harold G. Schrier, Twenty-eighth Marine Division, was given a small flag (58" x 28") to plant at the top when the patrol had completed the climb. Once there, they located a long pipe. Lindberg, along with others, mounted the flag to the pipe. After the pipe was placed in the ground, Marine photographer Lou Lowery snapped the photo with the men proudly gazing at the stars and stripes. Lindberg was one of the group.

Four hours later, the first flag was taken down and a second, much larger flag (96" x 56") was raised by a different group. Associated Press photographer Joe Rosenthal captured the moment with his camera.

In the meantime, Corporal Lindberg had gone down to replenish the supply of fuel for his flame thrower, unaware of the second flag raising. His platoon continued north on the island. On D plus eleven, he was wounded as he tried to knock out an enemy mortar position on Hill 362-A. He stated, "[K]nock out one pillbox, they get you from the next one. They were interconnected by tunnels. At one point, it took three days to advance the distance of a block and a half." Corporal Lindberg was awarded the Silver Star medal for heroic action. As the lone survivor of the first flag raisers (none of the second are alive), he feels that too much has been made of the men raising the flags. He said, "Every Marine who fought on Iwo helped raise those flags and nobody deserves special attention."

The photo of the first flag raising was not as dramatic as the second. The first shows Marines standing around the smaller flag. Its distribution was rather limited to the Marine Corps and *Leatherneck Magazine*. It did not get the coverage of Rosenthal's photo, which had worldwide distribution and immediately captivated the public and the media with this inspiring chapter in our nation's glorious history.

It must be stated that, according to military protocol, the American flag is raised after control of the island has been gained and the enemy's organized resistance has been eliminated. Consequently, the raising of the first and second flags over Mt. Suribachi was contrary to regulations. That, however, did not negate the powerful, positive impact the sight of "Old Glory" had on the troops still fighting to the north. The battle would continue for weeks.

On March 14, Lt. Gen. Holland M. Smith, commanding general of the expeditionary troops on Iwo Jima, declared that organized resistance was no longer a threat. A flag was raised at Kitano Point at the northern end of the island to mark the event. This was the official flag raising on Iwo Jima. An official Marine Corps photograph taken by T.Sgt. James A. Mundell shows Lt. Gen. Holland M. Smith and Maj. Gen. Graves B. Erskine of the Third Marine Division with the troops looking on. This photo and the Kitano Point flag raising itself are not well known. The setting was rather obscure and modest. On the same day, the Mt. Suribachi flag was removed. Though official, the third flag raising did not receive its due recognition. No photo of Iwo Jima could compete with Associate Press photographer Joe Rosenthal's Pulitzer Prize–winning shot.

While recuperating in the hospital at Aiea Heights, Hawaii, we heard that, initially, sources in Washington were displeased over the infraction of protocol regarding the premature raisings of the flag on Mt. Suribachi. The tremendous positive response of the Associated Press photograph, however, overshadowed the seemingly minor breach of military protocol. The famous photo generated renewed public spirit and uplifted morale at home. Consequently, any form of reprimand would have been counterproductive to our cause.

Three of the six men in the Associated Press photo were killed later during the battle, and the survivors were called back home for a national tour to promote the sale of war

The third—and official—flag raising on Iwo Jima occurred March 14, 1945, when organized resistance had been neutralized at Kitano Point at the northern end of the island—a little-known fact to the public and some historians as well. Lt. Gen. Holland M. Smith, commanding general of the expeditionary troops on Iwo Jima, *right,* and Maj Gen. Graves B. Erskine, of the Third Marine Division, joined the troops to witness the event. The battle of Iwo Jima officially ended on March 26, 1945.

bonds. They were acclaimed America's heroes and became instant celebrities.

The first mail drop occurred on or about March 1. Mail was distributed to the troops as their units were relieved on the front lines and they were sent to a relatively safe area to the rear for a brief breather before returning to the front.

Since all of my company's superior officers had been killed or wounded on our first day of combat, it became my duty, among other responsibilities, to distribute the mail to our men. The bulk of this mail from home had been written prior to the date of our landing, so the writer did not know the letter would be read on Iwo.

By March 1, our losses were well over 50 percent. By the time of our next mail drop, K Company had been reduced from 230 men to about 40. As I looked at the names on the envelopes, I called out only the names of those who were still there. The others were placed in a container to be returned to sender.

The men were obviously anxious to hear their name as I read them. When they saw most of the letters landing one by one in the container, they felt the impact of the loss of their buddies. I saw it on their emotionally drained faces and I'm sure they witnessed it on mine.

The purpose of distributing mail from home was to lift our spirit and morale. At times it had the opposite effect, particularly in the letter received by Lt. Red Baker, about his twin being killed in Germany. I learned later on that some of the letters were "Dear John" letters. Receiving bad news is always troublesome, but how much more so to the recipient who soon will return to confront the enemy.

On return flights from bombing Tokyo, our superforts dropped their unexpended bombs on Iwo, striking prime targets. Flight cameras clearly showed the destruction of specific targets, such as an antiaircraft emplacement destroyed by a direct hit. The next day, however, the photographs showed the emplacement intact. This unexplained phenomenon occurred regularly at different targets.

The mystery was explained after we landed. We discovered that Lt. Gen. Tadamichi Kuribayashi's men had built wooden dummy emplacements as decoys. We blew them to pieces one day; they were replaced by the next day. We were under the impression that we were destroying the real emplacement. The actual antiaircraft guns and artillery emplacements, however, were embedded underground or in caves, undetected and protected.

Tokyo Rose (Iva Ikuko Toguri), a United States citizen born of Japanese parents, was in Japan at the outbreak of the war. Unable to return to the United States, she became a disc jockey for the Japanese-controlled radio network. Her mission was specifically to reach our men in the Pacific campaigns via short wave with American music, especially sentimental love songs that would make us homesick, thus demoralizing us.

Between songs, she strongly suggested with her tantalizing comments that the girls we left behind were unfaithful, that we were risking our lives for their new "draft-dodger" lovers. Most of us regarded her program as entertaining and would laugh it off, " . . . laughing on the outside, but crying on the inside," as the song says.

Tokyo Rose did, indeed, raise doubts in the minds and hearts of some of our men, according to the outgoing mail I censored. She succeeded in provoking feelings of concern for those who were married or romantically involved. Also, a few of the men in K Company received "Dear John" letters. On a lighter note, one of our men wrote the exact love letter to five or six girls back home. More than once I had to advise him that he had inserted a letter to one girl in an envelope that was addressed to another.

What concerned me more was the accuracy of Tokyo Rose's reports relating to our military movements. When we left Guam for Iwo, we learned of our destination first from her, and then from our commanding officers. She told the Third, Fourth, and Fifth Marine Divisions that the Japanese knew we were on our way and that they were prepared to extend a cordial welcome upon our arrival. She mentioned units, their location, and troop movements, as well as dates.

She told us that some of our cities had been bombed, resulting in massive destruction and heavy loss of life; that the emperor's troops had landed in California and had us on the run; that the West Coast was blocked and our ships could not enter or leave our ports; that the Japanese were holding our women and children prisoners, etc. etc.

Tokyo Rose was arrested after the war and released in 1946, but in 1948 she was rearrested, charged with treason, and convicted. She was sentenced to serve ten years in a federal prison and fined ten thousand dollars. She served six years and was released in 1957. Pres. Gerald Ford pardoned her just days prior to his leaving office in 1977.

After V-J Day Maj. James Devereux, the hero of Wake Island whose cry "Send me more Japs" had inspired me to enlist in the Marine Corps, was released from a prisoner-of-war camp and was honored at various public functions across the United States. One of these occurred in my hometown of Jersey City. The program was organized by Judge Alexander Ormsby, World War I Marine and former national commander of the Marine Corps League. The judge had invited me as a guest. I was still in uniform and when I arrived, I was assigned the seat next to Major Devereux (now a colonel). It was an unexpected honor to sit next to a Marine legend. At a loss for adequate words to start a conversation, I finally mustered enough courage to break the ice. I turned to him and said, "Colonel, I want you to know that it was your famous statement of 'Send me more Japs' that motivated my enlistment in the Marine Corps." He looked at me with an expression of disbelief, hesitated, and replied, "Lieutenant, why would I ask for more Japs? We had more than we could handle."

While on Guam I received a letter from Eugene Wanicki, a nine-year-old boy in a Catholic school in Chicago. He explained that his nun had the entire class pray for different servicemen overseas and that he had been assigned to pray for me. He sent a picture of himself in his Communion suit, and we began to exchange letters. He told me about himself, his family, and his school. This went on for some time, but after the war we lost contact. Now, after all these years, I still remember his name and still have his Communion picture. I don't know if it was my mother's prayers, my own, my guardian angel, or the prayers of Eugene Wanicki that saved me. Perhaps it was all of them. But of one thing I am certain, God does listen—and he does answer.

It seemed to me that God must have been with us on Iwo because I observed incidents exemplifying that greater love hath no man than he who is willing to risk his life for his fellow man, those who try to save their lives will lose it and those who are not afraid to lose it will gain it. I also thought God must have been very busy there because many of us were communicating with Him at the same time. We experienced the spiritual encounter of a lifetime—perhaps not during the fighting, but surely in the lull periods during those endless nights.

Unlike other campaigns, on Iwo Jima we felt we were fighting a phantom. It was difficult to pinpoint the enemy because they moved from one cave to another through their connecting tunnels. Also, they used smokeless gunpowder, which afforded them concealment. We often felt that there were as many of them behind us as there were in front. Several of their positions had to be captured more than once.

In retrospect, I remember that Iwo Jima was so congested that if troops of both sides were to stand equidistant to each other with outstretched hands, our fingertips would just about touch.

The volcanic ash on Iwo was so soft I could dig a foxhole by scooping the soil with my bare hands. I also recall scraping a foxhole ten inches deep and getting into it, only to find the ground so hot that I jumped out. The ground still retained volcanic heat. I remember cold nights that would cause me to rotate my body because one side of me would be too cold and the other too hot. When we wanted to heat our canned rations, we would dig a small hole and bury the can for a few minutes to get it hot enough to eat. We would use our combat knife, similar to a hunting knife, or dagger, to open it; then the steam would spurt out as a geyser. After it cooled down, we would cut the top off the can and indulge in our one-course meal.

Two men, noncombatants, were very important in building and maintaining our morale; one was the chaplain, who responded to our spiritual needs and was constantly telling us each day as we progressed that we were near the end of the battle. "It won't be long now," he said every day. It was his daily prayer. The other was a service representative of the Salvation Army, who constantly came up to the front asking if he could be of assistance. I remember one cold night while on vigilance. The man came with a bucket of hot coffee and a ladle, going from one foxhole to the next. I never saw members of any other service organization risk their own lives as they comforted our troops. Other organizations played a role, but only the Salvation Army possesses a permanent hold on our gratitude.

Infantrymen ordinarily gain a sense of security when tanks are used to support them in an assault. This was not the case on Iwo Jima. The tanks attracted the greatest firepower that the enemy could dispatch. The maneuverability of our tanks and other mechanized equipment was held to a minimum because of the soft volcanic ash. Casualties ran very high in the tank units, and on Iwo we did not particularly welcome them as our support.

One afternoon while clearing caves in the northern end, we came across a large cave that contained several piles of wooden cartons. We shot the flame onto the cartons. They began to burn and we soon discovered we had hit the paymaster's cave. The wooden boxes contained Japanese currency. A strong draft from the tunnel carried the money high into the sky, then fell to the ground. I remember someone yelling, "It's raining dollars."

Near the northern end of Iwo, we entered a cave that contained boxes of ammunition. I noticed that some of them had the U.S. Army ordnance symbol with stamped dates of the 1930s. I wondered how and why they were able to obtain our ammo.

The Japanese had trouble pronouncing certain words, such as "yellow," "lemon," "lanolin," and others containing the letters *l* and *n*. As a result, we used such words as our password. Especially at night, when it was common to shoot at anything that moved, we would initiate the challenge by stating the first word, such as "rotten." If they did not respond quickly with "lemon," they would be shot. The password changed constantly. We had to use this system to determine whether that person moving in the dark was friend or foe.

Whenever we were wounded, we bled profusely and a tourniquet had to be used to stop the flow of blood. By comparison, the Japanese bled slightly when wounded. Hit by bullets or shrapnel, only a small amount of their blood oozed out. We were amazed by the contrast and surmised it might be due to the different inherent physiological characteristics or our distinctive diets. Nonetheless, their blood coagulated faster than ours, or our blood flow was more rapid. Pfc. Joe D'Amico suggested to me, "Maybe that's why it takes longer for them to die." Someone else retaliated, "Then we have to hit them with more bullets."

I noticed that shells from the enemy's field pieces were hitting in the same spot, while ours formed a pattern spraying a wider area. I'm not sure if the difference was in the calibration of the weapon or in the charge of the shell. Therefore, I tried to avoid jumping into a crater caused by their shell; the next one would fall in the same spot. We felt safer if we took cover between their shell craters, at least from their field pieces.

The Japanese had stored many bottles of sake, their alcoholic beverage. On Guam we came across a supply once in a while. Our superiors warned us that the sake may have been poisoned by the Japanese. We were cautioned against the temptation to drink it.

Mothers are known to worry about their sons, making certain they are well fed, clean, healthy, protected from harm, and in good company when away from home. On Iwo, we ate rations, we were not washed, we were subjected to enemy fire, and the Japanese were not good company. My mother, like others, stressed cleanliness. "Take a shower, change your socks and underwear everyday," she preached. We had no showers on Iwo, and we wore the same socks and underwear and slept on the ground. I remember thinking, "If she could only see me now."

Iwo Jima was expected to be a short, three-to-five-day battle, with provisions of food and supplies for two weeks.

It was disheartening to learn that Pres. Lyndon Johnson decided to return Iwo Jima to Japan. The island contains the blood of thousands of our men who valiantly fought and died for our nation. Although the remains of our heroes have been moved to American soil, Iwo Jima is an American shrine to be revered, not abandoned.

The Angel of Death was our constant companion throughout the campaign. He refused to abandon us.

I remember searching the enemy dead for possible valuable military information. It was with intense sensitivity that I went through the belongings of the dead enemy. I hoped for military data, but most often what struck me would be the pictures contained in their wallets. I would think, he belongs to someone back home: a wife, children, parents, all probably waiting for his return just as our families were hopeful of ours.

Yet just minutes before these men were trying to take our lives. I then visualized that the "someone" in Japan would soon receive notice that their loved one was killed in combat and not returning. It did not make sense.

The battle for Iwo Jima brought us within Japan's inner circle. We were knocking at the enemy's door. It was like getting down to their ten-yard line, where the defense stiffens and gaining yardage requires the utmost effort to cross the goal line. But we were not on Iwo for a game, and the casualties were not the same.

Throughout the world, Americans are known to place a high value on the collection of souvenirs. The Japanese knew this and booby-trapped many of their swords, rifles, and other glittering objects that they knew would attract our attention and arouse our curiosity. They even booby-trapped their dead, knowing we would search them for military documents. I was told two Marines from another company were enticed by the glitter of a Japanese sword at the opening of a cave. They made the mistake of investigating by entering the cave. They were not seen again. Our leaders stressed the best souvenir a Marine could take back home was himself.

Napalm is intended to demoralize the enemy, resulting in panic and disorganization. It was what we needed to repel the oncoming Japanese; it was not meant for us. It's sufficient risk to face enemy fire without having to contend with additional risk from one's own team. Yet, in the heat of battle and the ensuing confusion, it is conceivable that some of our men became unintended victims of "friendly fire."

Napalm bombs had a deleterious connotation for us. Nothing seemed so devastating as the threat of being hit by the acid spray of a napalm bomb that burned through

One of two cemeteries on Iwo Jima, where our fallen heroes were buried. In 1968, Pres. Lyndon Johnson returned the island to the Japanese government. All of the Americans' remains were removed to American soil. The victory of Iwo Jima was the costliest Marine campaign in U.S. history. As Maj. Gen. Graves B. Erskine said during the dedication of the Third and Fourth Marine Divisions' cemetery, "Let the world count our crosses. Let them count over and over. . . . One who did not fight side by side with those who fell can never understand."

clothing and flesh. Its victims screamed as they twisted and turned in agonizing pain caused by our own shells falling short. The rest of us could only stand by and helplessly watch. We were not prepared or trained how to help in this situation.

Moving to a new position as we advanced northward, we heard the screeching of missiles coming our way. I was next to 1st Sgt. William E. Moore. I dove to the ground; he went the other way and crawled under a disabled tank that appeared to offer more protection. At the conclusion of the barrage, I rose to appraise our losses and continue our advance. I looked at Sergeant Moore, who was still under the tank. I went to him. He was killed when a missile made a direct hit on the tank. I notified Colonel Boehm of the incident. It's a sad commentary; we had to leave him there. Our mission to join another company was our prime priority. There was no latitude for compassion or personal sentiment at such a time—that came later in retrospect.

Late in the campaign I noticed wireman Ishmael Gonzalez, of Chicago, having a heated discussion with a Marine from another unit. After the stranger left, I asked Gonzalez, "What was that about?" He said, "Oh, he wanted to borrow my wire cutters because he found a dead Jap with gold teeth, but I refused." I commended him for his humane decision.

I'm certain that anyone going into combat for the first time is apprehensive about how he will react. I know I wondered how I would hold up under fire. Will I freeze? Will I be afraid? Will I be ready to kill? Will I be killed? Will I be captured? These are normal concerns preceding the baptism of fire.

I saw no one run, nor did I hear of any, although two of our company suffered from initial shock and were escorted back to the ship for their safety as well as our own. They refused the option to sit out the campaign on the ship and rejoined K Company in a couple of days. When we saw them coming back to our line we gave them a rousing cheer.

I saw a Marine from an adjacent unit who was wounded and in obvious pain. He fell into a shell crater, which offered some concealment against further injury from the enemy. Another Marine ran to him. I could see he was talking to the wounded man, then picked him up to carry him. He ran but a few steps when he himself was hit. Both managed to crawl back into the crater. At that point K Company was ordered to move ahead. I never learned of the outcome of those two Marines. The heroics of jeopardizing one's own well-being for the safety and comfort of a wounded comrade was commonplace on Iwo.

There is a general misconception that there is glory in war, a myth that is generated by the media and Hollywood and fostered for pecuniary motives. The public has been sensitized to this sensational portrayal of war. War is not glorious. There is no glory in killing and bloodshed.

I don't know if it was a hallucination, a delusion, a fantasy, or perhaps a dream. A few days after I was evacuated to the hospital on Guam, I visualized we were crawling on our bellies, drifting aimlessly in different directions through dimly lit, smoldering, narrow, dirt tunnels crossing each other and going in circles. We came upon a murky valley with limited visibility, then back into the tunnels with numerous curves, looking for an exit that did not exist.

We were in a maze, wandering, moaning and groaning, grunting for direction, looking for someone or something, but no one knew. We were lost in an inescapable trap that seemed to capture or reflect the essence of Iwo's presence.

This eerie setting—a persistent, recurring nemesis—haunted me for a long time. It was a surrealistic experience, a nightmare in hell.

Index

Page numbers in *italics* refer to illustrations

Patrick F. Caruso was a native of New Jersey. He was educated at Western Maryland College and later earned two M.A. degrees from Seton Hall University. Eager to join the war effort, Caruso enlisted in the Marine Corps while still in college and attended officers candidate school at Quantico, Virginia.

After receiving his commission, he was assigned to the Ninth Regiment, Third Marine Division, and in February 1945, his company launched its attack on Iwo Jima. By the end of the attack, all five of Caruso's senior officers had been killed or wounded, leaving him in command of K Company. Before the battle was over, Caruso also was a casualty.

Following the war, Caruso was employed by the Veterans Administration as a rehabilitation officer assisting disabled veterans. In 1953 he began a career in education, retiring in 1981 after thirteen years as superintendent of the Morris Hills, New Jersey, district schools.

Caruso was also the author of numerous newspaper and magazine articles, including an Associated Press article commemorating the battle of Iwo Jima. His widow, Mary, lives in New Jersey and Florida.

Author Patrick Caruso in 1943, *left*, and in 1970, *right*, holding the Bible with the bullet hole that would have killed him if not deflected by a steel shaving mirror in his pocket (note hole in jacket pocket). Photo on left from author's collection; photo on right AP Newsfeature photo.